quisitions Editor: Mary B. Good
ior Managing Editor: Jack Kiburz
erior Design: Lucy Jenkins
ver Design: Jody Billert, Billert Communications
esetting: the dotted i

e Rhythm of Business™, Collaborative Community™, and Collaborative
mmunities™ are trademarks of The Rhythm of Business, Inc.

rary of Congress Cataloging-in-Publication Data
man, Jeffrey C., 1945-
    Collaborative communities : partnering for profit in the networked economy
/ Jeffrey Shuman and Janice Twombly with David Rottenberg.
      p.   cm.
    Includes bibliographical references and index.
    ISBN 0-7931-4435-3 (6x9 hardcover : alk. paper)
    1. Business networks.   2. Information technology—Economic aspects.
3.   Computer networks—Economic aspects.   I. Twombly, Janice.
I.   Rottenberg, David, 1946– .   III. Title.
HD69.S8 .S54 2001
58'.044—dc21
                                                    2001000506

collaborative communities

Partnering for Profit in the Networked Economy

Keep onda

Jeffrey Shuman and Janice Twombly

with David Rottenberg

The Rhythm of Business, Inc.

A **Kaplan Professional** Company

MORE PRAISE FOR *COLLABORATIVE COMMUNITIES*

"*Collaborative Communities* illuminates an emerging pattern of business development fundamental to success in the networked economy. It is clear, succinct, and accessible to anyone seeking an understanding of best business practice in the information age."

—Joseph Morone, President,
Bentley College

"In a global economy with intense world competition for every customer's dollar, companies must continually innovate. The brilliance of *Collaborative Communities* is that it describes a business model that incorporates innovation into its very core. It doesn't matter how large or small your company, Shuman and Twombly have written a formula for making every company entrepreneurial, customer focused, and profitable."

—Richard Slifka, Treasurer,
Global Petroleum Corp.

"Shuman and Twombly have written a breakthrough business book! It's filled with knowledge no one else has articulated. Any executive who wants to run a profitable business in the networked economy had better read this book."

—David P. Fialkow, Co-CEO,
General Catalyst

"*Collaborative Communities* is provocative. As the CEO of one of the profiled companies, the book reflects keenly on where our company has been and illuminates a roadmap for our future. If you want to understand the business model for the 21st century, *Collaborative Communities* should be number one on your list."

—Janet Kraus, Cofounder and CEO,
Circles

"*Collaborative Communities* builds a viable framework for understanding your customers and, most importantly, helps you evolve a business that will maximize your sales and profits. A must-read for anyone seeking to grow a business."

—Dr. Robert Ronstadt, Director,
IC² Institute

"The authors ask two fundamental questions every CEO should be obsessed with: Are you spending more time trying to build a specific business model when you should be putting in place an ongoing process that allows that model to evolve as customer needs evolve? Are you monetizing all your business relationships or just one or two? The book shows the way to excel in both these important areas."

—Larry Stybel, Cofounder and President,
Stybel Peabody & Associates, Inc.

"*Collaborative Communities* is both a visionary look at where business is going and a practical nuts-and-bolts guide on how new and veteran entrepreneurs can get there. From growing your business model to creating a collaborative community that can personalize your products and services, this book is a must-read."

—Christina Bauer, Founder and CEO,
Mindful Technologies, Inc.

"Yesterday's strategic advantages rapidly become millstones around your neck! You can no longer afford to keep everything you need on hand all the time, or to pursue every worthwhile opportunity. How can you gain sustainable advantage in today's shifting economy? *Collaborative Communities* offers valuable insights for us all."

—Michael I. Eizenberg, President and
Founder, eTrav.com

TO OUR MOTHERS,

Bertha Shuman, Elizabeth Twombly, and Rachel Rottenberg, for a lifetime of love and understanding.

Contents

Acknowledgments

Without a doubt, it took a collaborative community to write this book.

Clearly, the book would not have been possible without the thoughtful contributions of David Rottenberg, our editor at The Rhythm of Business, Inc., and valued collaborator in all our writing.

Stephanie Pierce-Conway's design talent allowed us to see and illustrate the community vividly (and sometimes humorously).

A special thanks to Stacey Glazer, who assists us in getting the words out by managing our communications, speaking, and training engagements.

Our thinking has benefited greatly from Buddy Carp, our friend and associate who has helped us make sure our theories are grounded in the realities of creating successful businesses.

A special thanks to Christina Bauer, R. David Newton, and Fred Tuffile, whose partnerships have helped us understand what it takes to build a successful collaborative community.

Our heartfelt gratitude to our customers, friends, and supporters—Doug Adams, Jon Aram, Joe Bardenheier, Bill Bayne, Stephen Berman, Eric Bobby, David Bryan, Matt Casey, Joe Cronin, John d'Arbeloff, Tim DeMello, Gordon Earle, Mike Eizenberg, David Fialkow, Jay Fialkow, Bruce Gallagher, Gary Geraci, Shayne Gilbert, Dennis Huang, Irwin Heller, Rakesh Kamdar, Alexander Karafilidis, Melanie Keveles, Daniel Krysiak, Christopher Leblanc, Eliot

Leblanc, Deborah Lira, Gregg Levin, Marijo McCarthy, John McDonald, Frank McDonnell, Sharon McDonnell, Andrew Merken, Kristin Moore, Lindsy Parker, Jeff Regen, Michael Sattler, Jim Savage, Jerry Schaufeld, Bruce Schwoegler, Henry Shterenberg, Richard Slifka, Jerry Socol, Arthur Stratton, Laurence Stybel, Gregory Sullivan, Tony Sutton, Michelle Toth, Greg Walsh, Steve Wintermeier, and Jason Wong.

Our special relationship with Bentley College is enriched by the unstinting support of Tony Buono, Pat Flynn, Charles Hadlock, Janet Mendelsohn, Joe Morone, Aaron Nurick, Lee Schlorff, John Seeger, and Hans Thamhain. In addition, hundreds of Bentley entrepreneurship students have sharpened our thinking with their questions and their answers!

Janet Kraus at Circles earned our deepest gratitude by so willingly allowing us into her collaborative community. Without the examples gleaned from her company, we could not have demonstrated our thinking with such clarity and passion.

The enthusiastic support of our agent, Doris Michaels, and her staff helped our manuscript find a truly innovative publisher.

Mary Good, acquisitions editor at Dearborn Trade, and Robin Nominelli, director of marketing, made indispensable contributions to the finished book.

And none of this would have been possible without the love and support of Jeff's family—Penny, Rachel, and Alison Shuman.

Preface

When I had the idea for my last book, *The Rhythm of Business,* it was a profound moment. In the few seconds it took for the insight to form, I realized I had discovered the intuitive process all natural-born entrepreneurs use to build and run a successful business.

Over the entire history of business analysis, the conventional wisdom has been that if you have an idea for a business and the idea is good and you implement the idea correctly, the business will succeed. If the idea is bad or you fail to implement it correctly, the business will fail.

In that moment of insight, I realized the conventional wisdom was wrong. In reality, no matter how good a business idea is, no matter how well the idea is implemented, as soon as you open your doors for business, you will find your business has to change—not just minor adjustments and small shifts in marketing or product design but *radical* change. Customers you never thought of will want your product, and customers you counted on will want your product in an entirely different form or, perhaps, not want your product at all.

In short, those people who succeed in business are not so much visionaries who devise products and services no one else has ever thought of and that millions of people suddenly desire, but rather flexible, information-alert individuals who understand what their customers tell them and can quickly respond by shaping their business to profitably provide that exact product and service.

This process (which is not as easy as it seems to implement) means that business and business thinking flow in cycles. Every cycle begins with an idea or assumption based on an initial level of understanding. The idea or assumption is put into practice. Then, the business environment, primarily in the form of the customer, responds. After that, based on the response, a new idea or assumption is created. This cycle repeats and repeats as any business grows and develops. But as you can see from the cycle, the chief skill is not being right in the initial idea or assumption. No one is ever completely right with their first assumptions. The skill is in the ability to gather information from the response and then incorporate that information into the next idea or assumption, which will necessarily be closer to what the customer needs and wants.

Having had this insight, I spent years verifying its truth from my own experience as an entrepreneur, observing the experiences of other entrepreneurs, and from my work as a professor and the director of entrepreneurial studies at Bentley College. Over and over, I found that The Rhythm of Business™ is the process.

Every successful business is developed in such cycles. Business writers and business thinkers (and even individual entrepreneurs) may obscure this fact by glossing over all the dead ends and misfires as inconsequential struggles before the right business ideas come. But, in fact, the dead ends and the misfires are what eventually produce the ideas that create the success.

This rhythm, The Rhythm of Business, is the process for developing and growing successful businesses of every size and every type, not just today but yesterday and tomorrow. It is always the same process. But it is not always the same pattern. What is true is that different businesses grow from the same process!

Starting from the age of mass production in the 1910s to the age of mass customization in the 1980s and 1990s, to the age of personalization that we have now, business patterns change as the result of political, social, economic, and technological developments. These developments alter the needs and wants of consumers and also provide businesses with the means to fulfill those changing needs and wants. What doesn't change? The process. Again, every business starts with an idea or assumption. The idea or assumption is put into practice. The business environment, primarily in the form of the customer, responds. Based on that response a new idea or assumption is created. It is because of the political, social, economic, and technological developments that different business patterns grow out of the same process.

Living at a time when a major technological revolution is sweeping the globe—the shift to the networked economy where anyone can be instantaneously connected to anyone else—it is obvious that this major event is necessitating a change in business patterns. Communication and information technologies are producing more powerful consumers with more personal needs and wants. And yet, at the same time, communication and information technologies are providing businesses with the means to satisfy those personal needs and wants. But how? What is the new business pattern?

Considering The Rhythm of Business methodology and the new technologies, I had a second insight. The business pattern required for the 21st century is what I call the Collaborative Community™.

But as with any idea, the insight is the easy part. Ideas, when they do appear, always appear effortlessly. The hard part is developing the idea, dotting the "i"s and crossing the "t"s and verifying that the idea is indeed correct. And it takes years.

This book is the result of that insight and those years of hard work.

Jeffrey Shuman
January 2001
Newton, Massachusetts

Introduction

When we undertook the challenge of writing this book, we knew that it would require our looking at the current period of profound economic change from many perspectives. We knew that to accurately describe the significance of the technological revolution we are in the midst of, we had to tell the big picture. That is, we had to describe the very changed business landscape from 40,000 feet. And at the same time, we knew that what we were describing was such a profound change from the business mindset of the 20th century, we had to also describe the landscape from ground level: up close and personal.

In addition to the task of telling the story from two heights, we had to also describe what was happening from two viewpoints. We knew the technological revolution was both empowering consumers and enabling businesses and, as a result, changing almost everything businesspeople think to be true. This meant that in addition to looking at the implications of the new landscape from the conventional viewpoint—the viewpoint of business—we had to describe it from the viewpoint of the consumer, a viewpoint that, unfortunately, many businesspeople find uncomfortable.

But there is no choice. Communication and information technologies are causing a shift in the balance of power between business and consumers so significant that today consumers really do expect to get exactly what they need and want—where, how, when, and at the price they want to pay. Consequently, to be successful you must now sit in the customer's chair. You must use a different approach from the one you used in the past and design your business, not from the point of view of the CEO, but from the viewpoint of the customer. This point of view changes everything. It leads to a very different business pattern and many possible business models. Again, as we said in the preface, the process is the same, but the pattern is different.

Over the past three years, we and our colleagues at The Rhythm of Business, Inc., have worked with dozens of entrepreneurs and entrepreneurial companies to help them understand the implications of this new netcentric, customer-controlled economy and identify and put in place an iterative and collaborative business model for achieving success. These experiences, coupled with the experience of building our own company, have helped us understand what it really means to sit in the customer's chair and develop a company from that point of view.

One of the challenges we faced in creating this book was figuring out how we could use new communication technologies to help our readers develop a better understanding of our subject. The problem is that while Internet time isn't quite as fast as first thought, the pace of business and technological innovation has quickened. However, given the lead time needed to publish this book in relation to how quickly businesses are changing, we wanted to find a way for the reader to continue to learn with us—even after the book was printed. So after some research, we decided to incorporate technology into the book that would enable our readers to stay in touch with us and continue to develop their understanding of how to achieve and maintain success in our new networked world.

To accomplish this goal, we decided to use two approaches: (1) include the Web site uniform resource locators (URLs) for a number of the companies we discuss and (2) use the new :CueCat technology developed by Digital:Convergence Corporation. Digital Convergence's :CRQ software and the :CueCat reader are *free* and do not require you to purchase any hardware or pay any user fees.

To obtain your free :CueCat reader, simply e-mail us at rhythm@ rhythmofbusiness.com, and we'll take care of the rest, or you can visit <www.digitalconvergence.com> to learn of other options.

Once you're :CueCat enabled, you can quickly link to supplemental material directly related to the concepts, companies, and technologies talked about in this book. Even more important, because these are "live" links, we can update the material. Instead of just reading this book and then closing the covers as you might have in the 20th century, we can now make this a continuing living story, and, if you choose, you can receive new information regularly. As you read the book, you will see :Cue symbols like the one below (which links to our Web site). By scanning the code into your :CueCat and uploading it to your computer, you will automatically link to the URL embedded in the code.

Enjoy the dance!

PART ONE

The Revolution in Business

It's Friday at 7 PM. You've just closed the biggest deal of your life, and you're sitting in the afterglow, musing about that Ford Thunderbird. You've waited a long time to buy your dream car personalized to your liking. So using your cell phone, you log on to Ford's Web site and scroll through to check what exists at any dealer or is ready to roll at a factory. If you find the car, it's trucked to you. If no model has the exact features you're looking for, you click on what you want. Your car, personalized exactly the way you specified, is assembled and delivered within seven days.

The Challenge

We live at the dawn of an economic transition as profound as the beginning of the Industrial Age. At the start of the 21st century, advances in communication and information technologies are driving a shift in power away from business toward consumers. Consumers are accessing information in quantities and at speeds that before were available only to large organizations. Exchanges of information at unprecedented levels of detail are now possible between consumers and businesses. Consumers are more powerful because they have control over to whom they give information and with whom they choose to do business. For almost every product and service, competition is not local or national—it's global. This increase in consumer power and the ability of anyone to share information with anyone anywhere at anytime is rapidly altering the way business must operate.

THE NETWORKED ECONOMY

If you're still not sure the so-called new economy is real, just listen to the change in thinking that has taken place at Ford Motor Company. Speaking at Dell Computer's DirectConnect Conference in September 2000, Jacques Nasser, president and CEO of Ford, exclaimed:

Customers determine everything. Thanks to the Internet and the instantaneous flow of information, customers are more knowledgeable about companies, products, and services than at any time in history. And when customers get ready to buy, they now have more options than ever before, thanks to an increasingly borderless, connected world. The customer is totally in charge, totally in command, and determines the future for all of us.[1]

Clearly, Nasser's statement indicates just how different the world of business is today than it was 90 years earlier when Henry Ford told his Model T customers, "You can have any color you want as long as it's black."

As you might expect, it's not just Ford that has had to rethink its relationship with its customers. The traditional business model is being flipped on its head. Until now, companies have told consumers what was available and at what price. Soon a consumer's personal shopping "bot" will tell a company what the consumer wants and what price the person is willing to pay.

The real implications of the changed relationship between consumers and businesses are only starting to be understood. At the Dell Conference, Ford's Nasser went on to say, "The old distinctions that define what a company does are becoming more difficult to outline. Am I the CEO of a motor company, or am I building wireless, mobile consumer services?"[2]

Actually, the impact on Ford, and for that matter on all companies, is much more profound than just how Ford defines what business it's in. In a *Business 2.0* interview, Peter Drucker, the preeminent business philosopher of the 20th century, stated: "The corporation as we know it, which is now 120 years old, is unlikely to survive the next 25 years. Legally and financially yes, but not structurally and economically."[3]

Perhaps there's no better example of the turmoil that advances in communication technologies have wrought than the situation at AT&T:

After more than a century of binding America together with sound waves and wire, AT&T Corp., once the country's biggest, wealthiest, and strongest company, is itself unraveling.

The story of AT&T's 115-year rise and fall illustrates two simple lessons of American capitalism. The first is that no company, however large and prosperous, is safe from the convulsions of social, economic, and technological change.

The second lesson . . . When Ma Bell lost its local service, it lost a vital connection to its customers, millions of employees, and the marketplace.[4]

WHAT HAS CHANGED?

When we think about business we think automatically about traditional corporate and industry structures that had their birth in the Industrial Age. These traditional structures were very successful in accomplishing their goals. No one can deny that traditional corporate and industry structures have fed, clothed, housed, transported, and entertained billions of people for decades. But the very technology these structures created has spawned a new generation of information and communication systems that are now rendering the corporation, as we know it, obsolete.

Look at the turmoil in the publishing industry with authors like Stephen King releasing books electronically, while Charles Schwab has redefined what a successful financial services company should look like. In the music business, peer-to-peer technology is fundamentally changing the record industry. And for that matter, these content-management advances are being combined with significantly enhanced wireless delivery mechanisms to alter the way digitized content changes hands. Technology is not only revolutionizing the music, movie, financial services, and publishing industries, but also bringing gut-wrenching change to any industry that has a product or service that is easily digitized.

In the era of mass production, a vertically integrated corporation was the most suitable business model. In the era of mass customization, corporations outsourced a lot of their manufacturing needs and the reigning business model was the virtual corporation. But the trillion-dollar question is, in an era when a powerful consumer is demanding personalized goods and services, *What is the business pattern best suited to* profitably *satisfy those individual needs and wants?*

Many of today's leading business gurus have recognized the need for a new way of conceptualizing, organizing, and structuring companies. Fortunately, the new technologies that have raised the expectation level of consumers are also helping businesses to satisfy those raised expectations. Consequently, whether they are described as living organisms,[5] business webs,[6] or value nets,[7] these new business patterns are being positioned as the models for value creation in the networked economy.

BUSINESS MODELS MUST ITERATE

Even more important than trying to define and/or invent the latest business model du jour, business pundits are realizing that it isn't any one business model that's truly significant. Rather, it's putting in place a business model that can change as technologies and customers change.

Writing in *The Industry Standard,* Nicholas Carr, executive editor of the *Harvard Business Review,* commented: "Success on the Internet often requires leaping from one business model to another."[8] Then there's Gary Hamel, recognized by many as a leading strategic thinker, who proclaims in his best-seller, *Leading The Revolution,* "Business concept innovation will be *the* defining competitive advantage in the age of revolution."[9]

Yet despite all the attention these business thinkers are placing on changing business models, they don't seem to understand the full implication of their insights.

Having to change one's business model on the road to success isn't something new. It isn't just another phenomenon of the Internet. Success in business has *always* been based on satisfying customers' changing needs and wants. And building a successful business model to do that has *always* required using an intuitive and iterative business-building process fueled by learning from paying customers.

What's surprising is that the idea is treated with such surprise.

Marketing guru Patricia Seybold, in a recent article, profiles several e-businesses that have had to change models to survive, even though, as she stresses, "None of them planned to alter their business models when they started out."[10]

The problem is that most people still think you can get it right the first time. Most people still think you can build a successful business based on the idea on which you launched your business, if the idea is good enough. And, of course, if you didn't think your idea was good enough, you wouldn't have launched your business.

Oh, sure, everyone expects bumps along the way. Everyone expects tweaks and adjustments will have to be made. But no one expects radical change. No one expects to change the entire business. Yet to succeed in business, that is very often necessary. Why?

Because when you start a business, you have to make assumptions, and assumptions are not facts. Your business has not started. You do not have any feedback from paying customers. And even if you have a working business and real feedback, you still have to interpret that information, and the information is always changing because customers and their needs and wants always change.

SUCCESS IN BUSINESS

This point is important so let's be clear: Success in business is not a function of your company's business model. Rather, achieving and maintaining success requires that you put into place a process that allows your business model to evolve in such a fashion that it continually satisfies your customers' ever changing needs and wants on an increasingly personal basis. In fact, this iterative business-building process has become the only sustainable competitive advantage in this period of profound economic transition.

> The iterative business-building process is the only sustainable competitive advantage in this period of profound economic transition.

How do you put into place an iterative business-building process? By developing a business model that allows you to generate the information you need to make better and better assumptions. In other words, you attempt to develop a business model that satisfies your customers' needs and wants. Then you test the business model in the marketplace, learn from that test, and refine the business model to more accurately fulfill your customers' needs and wants. And you go through this process again and again and again.

It is important to understand that when you implement your business model, you are actually testing the assumptions on which the model is based. And you do that by keeping track of all the important metrics of your business that allow you to generate the information required to make better and better assumptions—who your customers are, what they need and want, and how well your business model is satisfying those needs and wants. In other words, when you "open for business," you use the information gathered and compare it against your assumptions. Wherever your assumptions are not valid, you revise them and modify your business model. Then you repeat this process continually.

This iterative cycle, this rhythm of business, dictates that change is an inevitable and inextricable part of every business. In fact, the dictionary defines *iteration* as "a procedure in which repetition of a sequence of operations yields results successively closer to a desired result." And that's exactly what your company must do. Unlike change, iterating your business model is not an unwanted and unexpected event. Iteration is *the* underlying process through which successful businesses are built, moving closer and closer, iteration after iteration, to satisfying your customers' needs and wants. So the idea that a business model has to change should never surprise. It should be planned for, because having to iterate your business model is not an isolated event. It is how successful businesses are built.

Think about it: If you had "perfect" information, you wouldn't have to make assumptions as you'd know your customers precisely, and therefore would know exactly how to satisfy them. However, because no one has perfect information, when in business you have to make decisions based on your current level of understanding. No matter how long you've been in business, customers and technologies are always changing and thus your business model must also change as your information and therefore your assumptions become more accurate.

ENTREPRENEURS LOVE TO HEAR
THE CASH REGISTER RING

Of course, change in business and in life presents us with the problem of timing. Timing, to be valuable, cannot be dictated, random, or haphazard. It has to be precise.

> Timing, to be valuable, cannot be dictated, random, or haphazard. It has to be precise.

In most business schools and business publications, the importance of timing is stressed, but unfortunately no one delves very deeply into the subject because no one feels competent explaining or teaching how to develop a sense of timing. Although timing is always to a certain degree intuitive, it can, however, in a very real sense, be taught and, in an equally real sense, developed.

Consider this example. Imagine an old-fashioned grocery store. It's Saturday. The grocer's out back, checking the stock. A high school kid is working the register. The store is small enough so that the grocer can hear the register even from the back room. It makes that nice old-fashioned sound. *Ka-ching. Ka-ching. Ka-ching.* Suddenly, the sound stops. The silence grows. The grocer wanders out from the back room to see what's wrong. The kid's still at his post, leaning on his hands, enjoying the break because the stream of customers is gone. The grocer immediately grabs a marker and some white cardboard and writes up a couple of un-advertised *Super Saturday Specials* and hangs them in the store windows. A few minutes later, the kid stops leaning on his hands and the *ka-ching, ka-ching, ka-ching* of the cash register is once again heard. Satisfied, the grocer returns to the storeroom.

That's timing.

Here's a quick updated version of the same story. During a conversation with an entrepreneur we were working with, we thought we heard his cell phone beeping. When we told him to feel free to answer his call, he surprised us by saying it wasn't a call. He had set his cell phone to buzz every time a customer ordered from his Web site. We couldn't believe it. Here he was 3,000 miles from his business and he was listening to his cash register ring! Clearly, *the key truths of business still hold.*

Of course, in both the old and new story, the entrepreneurs are really doing much more than listening to the cash register. They are, in fact, developing their ability to actually *feel* their business. Let's take a closer look at what we mean. Sure, every evening the grocer ran a summary of his cash register transactions: a printout of the total number of sales, the dollars of business he's done, the breakout of cash versus charges, the department where each sale was made, and so on. But as useful as those data are, in and of them-selves, they don't tell the whole story. Or for that matter, they really don't provide the grocer with his most important informa-tion: the flow of his business on a real-time basis that he can react to and change. Although the information in his cash register print-outs is valuable, it is at the *end* of the day. The ringing cash register provides the timing information at the moment the grocer needs to react to it that is missing in the printout. By consciously being aware of, and listening to, the time interval between rings of the register, the grocer can literally hear the rhythm made by the ring followed by silence followed by the next ring. In that way the length of the silence between rings is, in many respects, more useful than the ring itself because it allows him to actually hear the patterned flow of the *ka-chings*. That is, he can physically hear the rhythm of his business.

When the grocer stepped out of the storeroom to see what was going on, he was literally taking action based on the rhythm of his business. He didn't have to wait until that evening when he ran the totals and saw that sales for the day hadn't reached the level he expected. Instead, he took action in real time just as soon as he sensed the changed rhythm. And that's the point. Over time, the grocer is developing his ability to actually feel the rhythm of his supermarket to grow a profitable business.

Again, while the example of the grocer is simple, every business must identify and track its specific predictive metrics to allow it to assess whether its business model is achieving the results desired and, if not, to iterate its business model. In our simple example above, the frequency of the cash register ringing is the metric that tracks how well the customer acquisition process is working. Obviously, if the register doesn't ring frequently enough, the grocer is not attracting customers and thus some of the assumptions he's made about how to attract customers aren't valid and need adjustment.

Later on, we will discuss timing and how to develop it in more detail, but, obviously, the key timing issue is how long it takes you (or the grocer) to realize that your assumptions are right or wrong. How many rings do you have to hear before you decide to change your assumptions, or asked in a way we like better, how long do you have to wait between rings before the silence tells you that you have to change the assumptions underlying your business model? The quicker you can change your business model, the quicker you can attune your business to the needs and wants of your customers and the more profitable your company will be.

> The challenge facing all businesspeople today is to disregard their "legacy" thinking and start with a clean sheet of paper.

So, the challenge facing the leadership at Ford is the same challenge facing all businesspeople today: to disregard their "legacy" thinking and start with a clean sheet of paper; to begin with the consumer and then work through the value creation process, developing an understanding of when, where, and how value is created; and to then structure an iterative business-building process that allows businesses to profitably deliver personalized goods and services to their customers today and in the future.

To help you meet that challenge is the purpose of this book.

To Reiterate . . .

1. The increase in consumer power and the ability of anyone to share information with anyone anywhere at anytime is rapidly altering the way businesses must operate.

2. When we think about business, we think automatically about traditional corporate and industry structures that had their birth in the Industrial Age. But the very technology these structures created has spawned a new generation of information and communication systems that are now rendering the corporation, as we know it, obsolete.

3. Achieving and maintaining success requires that you put into place a process that allows your business model to evolve in such a fashion that it continually satisfies your customers' ever changing needs and wants on an increasingly personal basis. In fact, the iterative business-building process has become the only sustainable competitive advantage in this period of profound economic transition.

4. Iteration is *the* underlying process through which successful businesses are built, moving closer and closer, iteration after iteration, to satisfying your customers' needs and wants.

5. If you had "perfect" information, you wouldn't have to make assumptions because you'd know your customers precisely and therefore would know exactly how to satisfy them.

6. By consciously being aware of, and listening to, the time interval between "rings of the cash register," the businessperson can literally hear the rhythm made by the ring followed by silence, followed by the next ring. In that way the length of the silence between rings is, in many respects, more useful than the ring itself because it allows the businessperson to actually hear the patterned flow of the *ka-chings*. That is, the businessperson can physically hear the rhythm of his or her business.

7. The challenge facing all businesspeople today: to disregard legacy thinking and start with a clean sheet of paper; to begin with the consumer and then work through the value creation process, developing an understanding of when, where, and how value is created; and to then structure an iterative business-building process that allows businesses to profitably deliver personalized goods and services to their customers today and in the future.

ENDNOTES

1. Transcript of speech by Jacques Nasser, "Five Rules of Change for E-Business," September 2000.

2. Dan Neel, "Ford CEO Nasser Outlines Five Rules of Change for E-Business," *InfoWorld.com*, 21 September 2000.

3. James Daly, "Sage Advice: An Exclusive Interview with Peter Drucker," *Business 2.0*, 22 August 2000, 139.

4. Cynthia Crossen and Deborah Solomon, "Once a Corporate Icon, AT&T Finally Yields to a Humbler Role," *Wall Street Journal*, 26 October 2000, A1. Reprinted by permission of the publisher via Copyright Clearance Center, Inc.

5. Arie de Geus, *The Living Company* (Boston: Harvard Business School Press, 1997).

6. Don Tapscott, David Ticoll, and Alex Lowy, *Digital Capital* (Boston: Harvard Business School Press, 2000).

7. David Bovet and Joseph Martha, *Value Nets* (New York: Wiley, 2000).

8. Nicholas G. Carr, "Giant Steps," *The Industry Standard*, 4 September 2000, 139.

9. Gary Hamel, *Leading The Revolution* (Boston: Harvard Business School Press, 2000), 18.

10. Patricia B. Seybold, "Making Changes in Midair," *Business 2.0*, 12 September 2000, 74.

2

The 20th Century

Business is going through a revolution! Companies and industries as we know them are ceasing to exist!

Statements like the one above are written frequently these days, but how do we evaluate if they are true? To answer the question, we need to understand the driving forces that have brought us to where we are now. In Chapter 1, we discussed the impact technological innovation has on both consumers and businesses. As a result of this impact, the interplay among businesses, technologies, and consumers is reinforcing customer expectations and increasingly empowering them yet simultaneously enabling businesses to profitably offer consumers just what they want, when they want it, and at the price they want to pay.

The increase in customer expectations obviously makes it more difficult for businesses to satisfy customers' needs and wants. But at the same time, technology increases companies' ability to profitably satisfy customers' heightened needs and wants. From this parallel development, we see that customer expectations and information and communication advances go hand in hand. Customers cannot expect what cannot be produced, but when items can be produced, customers will want them and corporations must produce them—and do so profitably.

Unfortunately, while technology is playing its role in aiding both consumers and businesses, existing business and industry models are standing in the way of making the personalization of goods and services economically attractive. Quite simply, the problem is that the business structures that prevail in our economy are not designed to fulfill the needs and wants of a knowledgeable and powerful consumer.

Throughout the last part of the 20th century, the approach that has shaped business has been incremental or evolutionary. But technology has brought us to a time when incremental or evolutionary approaches are no longer possible. Advances in communication and information technologies have so outdistanced the legacy thinking ingrained in the strategies and structures of companies and industries that this thinking is limiting their growth. Like the dramatic climatic changes that caused the extinction of the dinosaur, due to technology, traditional industry and business structures are doomed.

> The legacy thinking ingrained in the strategies and structures of companies and industries is limiting their growth.

A CLEAN SHEET OF PAPER

As we said in Chapter 1, the challenge facing all businesspeople is to disregard how their business works today, stop trying to make incremental changes, and take out a "clean sheet of paper." This clean sheet of paper (see Figure 2.1), the chief tool of the entrepreneur, can be daunting to a business with millions or billions invested in strategies and structures. However, it is a liberating tool to an entrepreneur who understands the iterative process of building a business. But daunting or not, the clean sheet of paper and the iterative approach must become one of your company's core competencies if you want to succeed in the networked economy.

Everyone has a mindset about business and industry today that comes from the past 100 years. When we think about business,

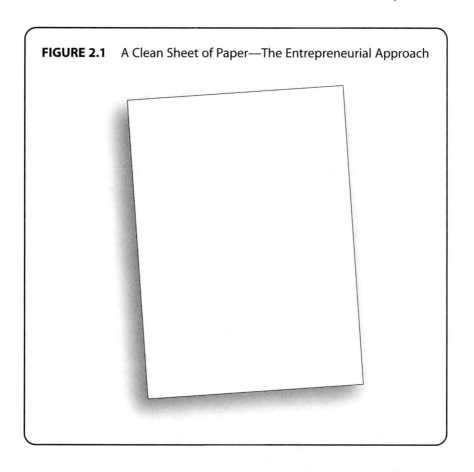

FIGURE 2.1   A Clean Sheet of Paper—The Entrepreneurial Approach

we think automatically about traditional corporate and industry structures such as manufacturers, wholesalers, and retailers or automobiles, telecommunications, and consumer products, all of which had their birth in the Industrial Age. These traditional corporate and industry structures were the dominant business paradigm of the 20th century. Although *paradigm* is one of the thousands of business buzzwords that have entered our vocabulary over the past several years, it is helpful to step back and understand just exactly what the word means. Scientific historian Thomas Kuhn has called a paradigm "an accepted model or pattern" that establishes an informational framework and set of rules by which its practitioners view the world.[1] But when the informational framework is challenged, that is, when the accepted model no longer provides an effective response, it is time for a new paradigm. In other words, once the assumptions on which the accepted model has been built are no longer valid, new assumptions must be made.

We've introduced the notion that the only sustainable competitive advantage in the networked economy is the process through which a company can iterate its business model as customers and technology change.

The ability to do that is based on your ability to quickly recognize the patterns you see as you gather information from customers, employees, partners, and suppliers. Indeed, in all of your interactions, you must assess the validity of your critical assumptions and make the necessary changes based on what you are learning on a real-time basis.

DEVELOPING UNDERSTANDING

Assumptions are your beliefs based on your current level of understanding. And as you learn from putting your assumptions into practice, your level of understanding will improve and you'll make better assumptions. This iterative process of learning (Figure 2.2) is universal. In business, it applies not only to an individual entrepreneur's business model but also to corporate and industry structures.

Yet when you are caught up in the day-to-day realities of a business, it can be very difficult to recognize just how fundamentally your assumptions need to change. A paradigm can be very useful for organizing information and setting priorities, but it can also filter out any information that is contrary to its framework. If your world view is one that says customers don't know what they need and want, think again. The increasing power of the consumer in the business-consumer relationship can no longer be ignored and is so significantly changing profit formulas that to continue to be successful, companies of all types must embrace the clean sheet of paper and develop a new set of assumptions to put into practice, learn from, and then refine.

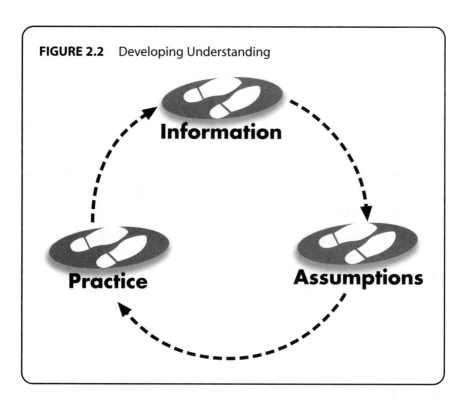

FIGURE 2.2   Developing Understanding

THE HISTORY OF CHANGING BUSINESS PATTERNS

Beginning in the latter half of the 19th century and gathering steam at the hands of Henry Ford and his production engineers, the system of mass producing to large, homogeneous markets became the dominant pattern of business. The Industrial Revolution created the technological environment for this structure, as described by Frederick Winslow Taylor in his book *The Principles of Scientific Management* published in 1911.[2] Taylor, who is considered the father of the scientific method of management, developed some of the initial frameworks for mass production that in essence have been followed ever since. In fact, mass production became virtually the only system of production practiced by large U.S. manufacturers.

When the age of mass production began, a huge pent-up demand existed for goods. Consumers weren't concerned whether they could get an icebox that was red. They just wanted an icebox. Henry Ford's famous saying, "You can have any color you want, as long as it's black," personifies the early days of mass production. And while today we laugh at that limitation, that Ford could mass-produce reliable Model Ts and Model As in sufficient volume to sell them for less than $300 was enough. Color didn't matter. It was beyond customer expectations.

Consumers were willing to accept standardized goods, for they brought with them unheard of convenience at prices everyone could afford. And accepting standardized goods helped increase sales for the companies that produced them, reducing prices even more through economies of scale. The result created a growing gap between the cost of craft goods made to order and the cost of goods mass-produced. This gap served to increase the sales of mass-produced or homogeneous products. In other words, consumer behavior reinforced the mass production model and led the practitioners of mass production to believe they had validated their assumptions and that profits would soon follow, as indeed they did.

Mass production led to the rise of vertically integrated corporations of which the classic example was Henry Ford's Rouge Center plant. This plant had coal, iron ore, and rubber trees going in one door, and Model Ts or Model As rolling out the other. Essentially, the Ford plant made every part of Ford's cars. "During its heyday in the mid-1930s, the Rouge employed more than 100,000 people, cranking out a new car every 49 seconds."[3] And that production system with very little change became the model of the ideal American corporation throughout the majority of the 20th century.

However, in the 1970s and 1980s, the relationship between corporations and consumers began to shift. The OPEC oil crises in the 1970s accelerated this change. Energy costs, and in particular gasoline costs, rose astronomically. As a result, the sale of fuel-efficient, Japanese-made automobiles skyrocketed. The boom in Japanese-made cars was but one of several factors that opened the gates to foreign competition in an ever increasing range of goods and services. Facing this sudden onslaught of cheaper, often better-made products, U.S. corporations were unprepared to compete, so after a recession and global humbling, American businesses began to transform their business models.

American management tried a number of approaches to regain market share, including process improvements within existing business models and borrowing from models they saw as successful, including the Japanese *keiretsu*. A *keiretsu* is a network of companies bound together by common interests, business relationships, and ownership. The *keiretsu* focuses on long-term strategy, controlling retail prices, and gaining market share without regard to short-term profitability.[4] This network of financially dependent companies provides for greater collaboration and thus specialization.

Vertically integrated mass production is totally different. Ford vertically integrated its operations because even though the fixed costs for setting up a factory system that involves transforming raw materials to finished goods are very high, once the fixed costs of the physical plant are covered, the profit on the next car coming down the assembly line is huge. So with very high volume, vertically integrated plants are very profitable.

Vertically integrated corporations mass-producing goods allow for a high degree of consistency and profitability. But not flexibility. Not a lot of things can change. For instance, every time you change color, you increase costs. Making all the cars black is much cheaper than painting them ten different colors.

As American companies began looking at foreign business models and particularly the Japanese *keiretsu*, a few of the buzzwords of the final quarter of the 20th century became *outsourcing, strategic alliances,* and *virtual corporations:* Don't do it yourself; outsource to a company with specialized expertise with whom you have likely developed a mutually beneficial relationship. By structuring a number of these relationships, you can also provide your customers with greater choice.

Under this thinking, Ford would approach another company and say, "We designed this radio or this steering mechanism. You make it for us." And over time, what happened is that instead of just telling suppliers to make a product or item according to their specs, Ford or General Motors says, "Well, you're in the sound-system business; you have that expertise. You come to us with what you think the sound system should be."

Companies began to very carefully assess *where* and *when* within the value creation process they were most effective and then focus on that as their core competence. So product design, the critical translation of customer requirements into product specifications, is just as likely to be run by a partner outside the four walls of the company as by a corporate VP—hence the term *virtual corporation*.

Over the past quarter-century, more and more companies have gone from doing everything in a fully integrated model to focusing on what they do best and aligning themselves with other corporations to do things they don't do well. DaimlerChrysler has 900 main suppliers. (By way of comparison, Dell Computer has only 25 main suppliers.[5]) Most American manufacturers will agree their manufacturing processes today are more accurately described as the assembly of components made by their outsourced partners.

The point we are making, however, is not about Ford or the automotive industry per se. Rather, it is that technological advances in production and information systems, along with economic and sociological changes, propel us from era to era. For example, the evolution from the mainframe computer to the minicomputer to the microcomputer and then to the Internet and now to wireless devices and the "Evernet" (the always-on, ever-present Internet) are, perhaps, the dominant technological advances that have ushered in change in the last half of the 20th century.

But as we've discussed, the same technological, economic, and sociological changes that affect industry also affect consumers. The ongoing relationship between the consumer and the corporation is like a dance. Sometimes the corporation leads, sometimes the consumer. When, for instance, due to a technological innovation, a company provides its consumers with choice, this choice that is intended to increase sales also strengthens the consumer. The consumer can now say no to a black car and demand one in red. And in the history of the 20th century, as technology increasingly made choice possible for the consumer, industry found itself making a transition from the era of mass production to an era of mass customization.

Vertically integrated corporations sell their mass-produced products into mass markets through mass communication channels by grouping the consuming public into major categories or segments, usually based on demographic and psychographic variables that are intended to be definable, measurable, and sustainable. These consumer profiles use such categories as males 40 to 54 years old who live in the suburbs and earn over $50,000 a year. Once a corporation identifies and describes such a group, it attempts to sell them a product. Moreover, once the corporation knows the makeup of the group, implicit in that knowledge is a method of reaching them. The corporation knows, for example, that men tend to read sports and automobile magazines. Women may read those magazines, but a whole set of other magazines focused on interior design and fashion are targeted primarily for women, and these magazines are very successful at reaching their intended audience. These profiling practices have flourished in the age of mass advertising. This is not to say that knowing customers on a more personal basis wasn't possible, even in the days of Henry Ford, but in terms of mass marketing, it is generally sufficient to think about customers as part of a large segment.

Broadcast advertising, especially the television commercial, is based on mass marketing concepts and is designed to sell mass-produced products. So in the United States and more and more everywhere in the world, we don't just have a business system, we have had an entire communications infrastructure based on the principles of mass production. And with good reason. It worked.

As we've pointed out, increasing technological innovation and global competition in the seventies and eighties increased customer expectations. Customers were more willing to say no to a prospective purchase because they understood that someone else was probably selling a similar product that better met their needs, perhaps at even a lower price. As consumers saw they had more choices, they quickly grew to *expect* more choices, and soon almost every industry was producing its products and services in a variety of makes, models, and styles. This variety ushered in the era of mass customization and the proliferation of product lines.

Although mass customization is an improvement over mass production, it still has strict limits. In other words, you can buy a product in different colors but only in certain preselected colors. An ad for Lenscrafters typifies mass customization. The ad claims you can get your prescription eyeglasses with the color and frame you select in one hour. However, even though Lenscrafters allows you to "design" your glasses by choosing from hundreds of frames, glass or plastic lenses, tinted or clear, bifocal or progressive, and so on, at the end of the day your ability to customize is limited to the *choices* Lenscrafters provides. You are not able to truly design your own glasses and have Lenscrafters make them for you.

Mass customization as a product design tool is so widespread we don't even realize it anymore. Adrian Slywotzky, Mercer Consulting vice president and author of several best-selling books, including *How Digital Is Your Business*, coined a phrase for a common method of mass customization: "choice boards."[6] To illustrate from the Lenscrafters example, you can assemble the exact combination of features you want but only from the options Lenscrafters makes available to you. That's a choice board. That's mass customization—a preselected range of alternatives available on a mass scale.

THE SHIFT TO PERSONALIZATION

Although the shift from mass production to mass customization may have taken decades, the shift from mass customization to personalization (the ability of consumers to dynamically reconfigure goods, services, and information to their liking) appears to be happening virtually overnight. In spite of our referring to mass customization and personalization as discrete capabilities, they are, in fact, points along a continuum that stretches from mass production at one end and individually personalized goods and services on the other. However, at some point along any continuum, a change that may be occurring becomes plainly visible; and for the purposes of this discussion, we have selected specific points of clear demarcation to serve as dividing lines. Today, we feel, enough change has occurred to clearly mark a transition from mass customization to true personalization.

Levi's now sells jeans that are manufactured for you based on a few key measurements. Lands' End creates a virtual model of your body from a computer scanner that measures 200,000 data points and is reportedly accurate to within one-eighth of an inch.[7] Avax Technologies is selling a personalized skin cancer vaccine in Australia in one of the first moves to market personal medicines.[8]

In the music industry, consumers no longer have to buy CDs with preselected cuts chosen by the recording company. If you want two cuts from Mozart, two cuts from Guns N' Roses, and six cuts from Buena Vista Social Club, technology allows you to download the music and burn the cuts into your own CD or your personal MP3 player.

And if you're like most Internet users today, you have personalized at least one news page, set up a personal stock ticker, and on and on.

Industries that are already digitized or have the ability to digitize, such as the financial, movie, and publishing industries, are undergoing immediate and radical change because they are among the easiest to personalize. But no industry is immune. The personalization of goods isn't absolute nor has it occurred in every industry, but to a greater or lesser degree, it is appearing in more and more businesses.

Even if a product seems difficult to personalize, such as the automobile with its high manufacturing costs so that mass production seems the only alternative, we find that because businesses are outsourcing so many of their product components, they can approximate the personalization of their product, as each company creates only a small part of the finished product. Where before the automotive industry would install seats that fit the average 40-year-old man, now we have seats for people with bad backs, temperature-controlled seats, high seats, low seats, and even personally contoured seats.

When people first look at product personalization, particularly in industries like the automobile industry, they say it's never going to predominate as a production model because of the cost. Personalizing a $40,000 SUV is a very different undertaking than burning your own CD. It seems a very expensive way to do business compared with mass production and mass customization. But even though the cost structures clearly are different, some of the old expenses of mass customization and mass production, such as the cost of inventory, are reduced with personalization.

Inventory exists because of the absence of information. Because a company doesn't know when or what customers are going to buy, they have to stock a large inventory. But large inventories of goods carry the risk of high manufacturing, storage, and shipping expenses as well as waste. If Levi Strauss has to make women's jeans in many different styles and sizes, it will have many returns and many unsold pants. But even though a customized pair of jeans may cost more to make, the extra cost is made up by the fact that the pair of jeans is in essence pre-sold. There is no inventory. Every pair of customized jeans that is made is already sold.

Dell Computer is a prime example of a company that is moving toward personalization profitably. In the Dell consumer-direct model, a customer orders a computer online or on the phone. From the computer or phone, the customer then configures the order by using choice boards. The use of choice boards isn't complete personalization, but the number of potential computer configurations is in the millions. Nonetheless, despite the variety of offerings, the system frees Dell from an inventory of completed machines. For that matter, the system also frees Dell from inventorying most component parts. Dell waits until someone places an order for a computer; that is the signal that triggers the information to Dell's component suppliers, who ship on a just-in-time basis the specific components needed. So, essentially, all Dell has to do is assemble the components, ship the completed computer, and listen to the cash register ring.

In looking back over the preeminent business paradigms of the 20th century, it's clear, as summarized in Figure 2.3, that advances in technology have been a dominant factor in establishing the relationship between business and consumers and in creating the prevailing business and industry structures that have profitably satisfied consumers. In the age of mass production and mass communication, consumers had little information or alternatives and thus accepted standardized goods and services. As more and more alternatives became available, consumers began to demand more so that to retain profitability, companies made incremental changes in the way business was done, as exemplified by the transition from vertical integration to virtual corporations.

However, as technical advances accelerated over the last part of the 20th century and businesses offered consumers such astonishing access to information and choice, consumers, believing their selection is infinite, increasingly want personal solutions to their needs and wants. And as it has in the past, technology is supporting those desires by providing more and more companies with the means to produce personal solutions. The economics of personalized goods and services are not the economics of mass production. Nor are they the economics of the preindustrialized craft system when most goods were personalized by hand. They are the economics of the technological age of personalization,

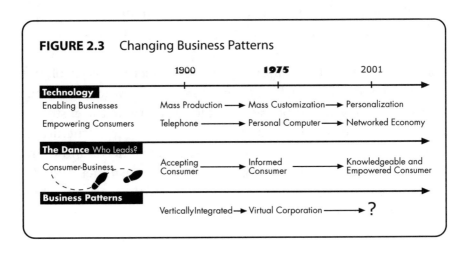

FIGURE 2.3 Changing Business Patterns

and the challenge for businesses is to develop an understanding of how to profitably satisfy each customer, one at a time.

When business leaders and pundits look at the shift from mass customization to personalization, they often think of personalization as simply the extension of a technological trend. But viewing personalization as simply a valuable technological trend is a mistake. The significance of this shift is not on the level of technology. It is on a much deeper and more profound level. The major shift taking place has to do with *who* determines the choices available. For instance, although choice boards are described as a "tool" of personalization, the user is limited to the preselected range of alternatives made available most often by the business on a mass basis. Personalization, on the other hand, increasingly empowers consumers to make the choices by dynamically reconfiguring goods and services to their liking. The second cycle of the networked economy is defined, not by what choices a business makes available to its consumers, but by the choices the individual consumer *demands* businesses make available to him or her. In other words, the shift in the continuum is on the level of the change in power between the consumer and the corporation. Per-

> The second cycle of the networked economy is defined by the choices the individual consumer *demands* businesses make available to him or her.

sonalization marks the point where the customer is in control, not the corporation. Personalization marks the point where the focus of every business has to be based not just on serving the customer as part of its mission statement, but where the very structure of the company is built around serving the personal needs and wants of its customers. Collaboration between the customer and the business is what provides the business with the understanding that makes personalization possible.

That level of change requires a new set of underlying assumptions for creating value for customers, employees, shareholders, and partners. In a networked economy, where information is freely available and a company across the globe is just as much a competitor for the consumers' dollar as the company next door, incremental change is not enough. Industrial Age models have been bent and twisted for decades. We need new models.

To Reiterate . . .

1. Technology is both empowering consumers and enabling businesses to fulfill customers' heightened expectations. As a result, the interplay among businesses, technologies, and consumers is reinforcing customer expectations and increasingly empowering them, yet at the same time enabling businesses to profitably offer consumers just what they want, when they want it, and at the price they want to pay.

2. Advances in communications and information technologies have so outdistanced the legacy thinking ingrained in the strategies and structures of companies and industries that this thinking is limiting their growth.

3. The increasing power of the consumer in the business-consumer relationship can no longer be ignored and is so significantly changing profit formulas that to continue to be successful, companies of all types must embrace the clean sheet of paper and develop a new set of assumptions to put into practice, learn from, and then refine.

4. Technological advances in production and information systems, along with economic and sociological changes, propel us from era to era.

5. The second cycle of the networked economy is defined, not by the choices a business makes available to its consumers, but by the choices the individual consumer *demands* businesses make available to him or her.

6. Personalization marks the point where the focus of every business has to be based not just on serving the customer as part of its mission statement but on building the structure of the company around serving the personal needs and wants of its customers. Collaboration between the customer and the business is what allows the business to have the understanding that makes personalization possible.

ENDNOTES

1. Thomas S. Kuhn, *The Structure of Scientific Revolutions,* 2d ed. (New York: New American Library, 1986), 19.

2. Frederick Winslow Taylor, *The Principles of Scientific Management* (New York: W.W. Norton, 1967, originally published in 1911).

3. Joann Muller, "A Ford Redesign," *Business Week,* 13 November 2000, 79.

4. <www.britannica.com/bcom/eb/article/0/0,5716,109540+10+106451,00.html?query=keiretsu>

5. <www.thestandard.com/article/display/0,1151,19351,0000.html>

6. Adrian J. Slywotzky, et al., *How Digital Is Your Business?* (New York: Crown Business, 2000), 39.

7. Rebecca Quick, "Getting the Right Fit—Hips and All," *Wall Street Journal,* 18 October 2000, B1.

8. Laura Johannes, "Avax to Sell Personalized Skin-Cancer Vaccine," *Wall Street Journal,* 18 July 2000, B1.

3

Dawn of a Revolution

Ith the drawing to a close of the 20th century, we witnessed the dawn of the Internet Revolution. But as with most revolutions, while everyone knew something important was happening, no one knew exactly what it was or how to take advantage of it.

The following three sketches take us through the dawn of the revolution and bring us to the point where we are now: to where incremental change in business has run its course; to where advances in technology must break through legacy thinking; to where the customer is in control and business must find new models to satisfy the needs and wants of customers on a personal basis.

However, before we can find new models for the 21st century, we need to understand the erroneous assumptions underlying those first Internet businesses and learn from their experiences.

WEDNESDAY, AUGUST 9, 1995

Wednesday, August 9, 1995, started out like any other day. But by day's end, the world as we knew it had changed. Forever. No, it wasn't because of some major geopolitical event. No wars were declared. Rather, it was because a California company named

Netscape, a leading maker of software used to navigate the Internet, offered stock in itself to the public.

At the bell, the company began trading at $71 a share, 154 percent above its offering price of $28 and more than twice the price the most bullish of analysts had predicted (Figure 3.1). Robert Natale, research director and new issues analyst at Standard & Poor's, described the overall reaction to the Netscape debut: "I have never seen this hoopla over an initial public offering . . . this has hit new highs in terms of excitement."[1]

FIGURE 3.1   Netscape Prospectus, August 9, 1995

NETSCAPE

Common Stock

Of the 5,000,000 Shares of Common Stock offered, 4,250,000 Shares are being offered initially in the United States and Canada by the U.S. Underwriters and 750,000 Shares are being offered initially outside of the United States and Canada by the International Underwriters. See "Underwriters." All of the Shares of Common Stock offered hereby are being sold by the Company. Prior to this offering, there has been no public market for the Common Stock of the Company. See " Underwriters" for a discussion of the factors considered in determining the initial public offering price.

THIS OFFERING INVOLVES A HIGH DEGREE OF RISK. SEE "RISK FACTORS" COMMENCING ON PAGE 6 HEREOF.

THESE SECURITIES HAVE NOT BEEN APPROVED OR DISAPPROVED BY THE SECURITIES AND EXCHANGE COMMISSION OR ANY STATE SECURITIES COMMISSION NOR HAS THE SECURITIES AND EXCHANGE COMMISSION OR ANY STATE SECURITIES ROSPECTUS. ANY REPRESENTATION TO THE CONTRARY IS A CRIMINAL OFFENSE.

PRICE $28 A SHARE

	Price to Public	Underwriting Discounts and Commissions(1)	Proceeds to Company(2)
Per Share	$28.00	$1.96	$26.04
Total(3).	$140,000,000	$9,800,000	$130,200,000

With a price of $71 per share, the company had a market capitalization of more than $2.7 billion.[2] At that time, very few initial public offerings had exceeded $250 million in market capitalization based on the pretrade offering price. Most had market capitalizations that were more in the vicinity of $100 million.[3]

Equally remarkable, the then 16-month-old Netscape had never posted a profit. In the quarter ending June 30, 1995, it had losses of $2.8 million on revenue of $14.1 million.[4] In comparison, when Microsoft made its initial stock offering in 1986 at $21, for that year, Microsoft, a company that first sought venture capital investment because Bill Gates wanted access to the network of contacts it brought, earned a profit of $39 million on revenue of $198 million.[5]

The Netscape shareholders smiling the widest on that warm summer day were certainly its top three executives. Chairman James Clark's 9.72 million shares were then worth $566 million; Vice President of Technology Marc Andreessen, a 24-year-old Internet hot shot and company cofounder, was worth over $58 million; and President and Chief Executive Jim Barksdale's 4.2 million shares were worth $245 million. The company's venture capital investors also had a huge payday. John Doerr, one of the most celebrated venture capitalists of the dot-com era and Kleiner Perkins Caufield & Byers partner, saw his 4.4 million shares reach a value of $256 million.[6]

In August 1995 the Web—or the World Wide Web, as it was then known—was often described as the graphically rich centerpiece of the Internet. With fewer than 10 million users, the Internet was still best known as a tool of the military and a way for academics to conduct research. In August 1995, only a very few people had the understanding to develop the tools needed to make commercial use of the Internet. The first wave of Internet entrepreneurs, starry-eyed geeks often thought to be social misfits, were just beginning to pound out code to create a new distribution channel for publishing, a new venue for financial services, and an extension of the traditional company's product catalog.

Interestingly enough, while the publishing industry continues to wrestle with the copyright issues inherent in electronic publishing, top-level publishing companies that were attempting to morph into "media companies" were among the private financiers of Netscape. Times Mirror Company, Knight-Ridder Investment Company, Hearst Corporation, and TCI Technology Ventures all reaped a huge payday along with the entrepreneurs and venture capitalists.[7]

Everyone was happy. Wall Street had voted with its wallet to develop commercial applications for the World Wide Web. Emboldened by Netscape's widely successful stock offering, dozens of Internet-related companies quickly filed for hoped-for lucrative public offerings. That expectation was fueled by investors' belief in the potential for phenomenal growth. At the time, online users were expected to more than double to 18 million, and $3 billion in revenues were forecast for the newly emerging industry.[8]

The Netscape stock offering caused a paradigm shift in the public equity markets. A company without profits had successfully offered its shares to the public. Before, companies went public only after seven years and four consecutive quarters of profitability. Netscape proved that stock market investors were willing to fund the growth of a new and exciting industry: the Internet.

Hand in hand, on August 9, 1995, entrepreneurs and investors entered the first cycle of the networked economy.

TWO TALES OF A CITY

Dickens was right. "It was the best of times, it was the worst of times." Only this time it wasn't the French Revolution; it was the Internet revolution. And it wasn't Paris or London. At the heart of this revolution was "Web City."

Everyone Wanted to Get to Web City

You know the place. As the first cycle of the networked economy ratcheted into high gear, everyone wanted to get to Web City (Figure 3.2). During the final half of the 1990s, a healthy market

FIGURE 3.2   All Aboard

for initial public offerings (IPOs) fueled the work of innovators who were reshaping old-line industries and even creating what was believed to be a new industry: the Internet. Buoyed by stories of the nearly overnight fortunes of Internet millionaires and even billionaires, such as Jeff Bezos of Amazon.com and Jerry Yang of Yahoo! to name but two, legions of newly minted MBA graduates, consultants, lawyers, and anyone with an idea for an Internet-based business headed to the Web, visions of the vast riches they would soon harvest dancing in their heads.

No matter what your role in the economy, you too might have wanted a piece of Web City. You too might have caught the start-up frenzy, looking for the *next big thing* to build a business around, wondering if you could become the next Internet billionaire.

Or perhaps you thought about going to work in a dot-com start-up, with dreams of stock options reaping you unheard-of wealth.

Or maybe you were seeking your fortune through investing in dot-coms. Stock trading became one of the first industries radically altered by the power of the Internet. Online brokerages such as E*Trade made it easier than ever to speculate on stocks and advertised heavily to encourage people to chase the pot of gold.

Entrepreneurs, stock analysts, and venture capitalists became the rock stars of the new economy.

In those early days, everyone was convinced gold was in those Internet hills, but no one seemed to know where or how to mine it. The conventional wisdom of the day held that all you needed to get rich.com was to have an idea for a Web-based business, write a good business plan, and find a venture capitalist or angel investor who would also believe; and you'd be on the IPO road to riches within 18 months (Figure 3.3). As time went on, there were ever more examples of nascent businesses, many without solid revenue models, cashing out as part of the dot-com frenzy.

The healthy economy meant that investors continued to pour money into the financial markets, primarily through tax-deferred

FIGURE 3.3   The Promise

y other—it will live or die on its ability to profitably deliver the perience customers want.

So whether it was the best or worst of times in Web City, all de-ended on which side of the IPO you lived, whether you bought ock or were issuing it.

FRIDAY, APRIL 14, 2000

Friday, April 14, 2000, was another day that started like any other spring day. By day's end, however, the world once more

---

retirement plans. As a result, big institutional investors such as pension funds invested in venture capital funds to boost their long-term returns, fueling an increase in available private equity to start businesses. And mutual funds were tending to buy more IPOs because they had more money to invest. The result: The retirement savings of Americans were providing the capital to fuel the development of companies that were in very early stages of growth and without proven business models.

As we reached the nadir of the first cycle in late 1998 and early 1999, the number of people around the world connected to the Internet continued to increase as did the demand for Internet products and services, the growth of electronic commerce, and the availability of capital. Developments in wireless communications, computer networking, and computer software made it seem as if this revolution in innovation would forever drive increases in the stock valuations of technology companies. Companies that went public used their highly valued stock to acquire new technologies, enlarge their customer base, and hire flashy management talent. A Ponzi scheme of inflated valuations began to play out.[9]

Profits? The "Numbers" feature in the November 1999 issue of *Business 2.0,* a popular business magazine of the new economy, confidently predicted "there is reason to believe that e-businesses that spend aggressively will emerge from the red if they can stomach the losses for six years or more."[10] Unfortunately, the reality was that the vast majority of Internet companies were not profitable because no one was asking them to be. Management skills were a plus but not necessary. After all, it is much easier to run a company if you don't have to be profitable. Of the more than 500 companies that had IPOs in 1999, a mere 25 percent could show a profit.[11]

One of the most glaring examples of suspended reality was the November 1998 IPO of theglobe.com, a community of Web sites. Despite minimal revenues and huge losses, the company's stock was offered to the public at $9 per share and quickly sky-rocketed to $97 on the promise of the riches that could be made by aggregating potential customers on a collection of Web sites.[12]

> The four building blocks of business are process, customers, information, and timing.

Process. Like many of their old economy counterparts, the first wave of Internet entrepreneurs assumed that they could "get it right" the first time. They assumed the business model they went to market with was ready for commercialization, and they spent millions on advertising and marketing to attract "eyeballs" that theoretically would become paying customers. That is, they believed that right out of the box they knew enough to put together the business that would satisfy their customers. For example, Barry Stouffer, a senior analyst at J. C. Bradford, said, "Webvan has done it the New Economy way: Raise as much money as you can and bet the ranch. They have determined in advance, without experience, that they have the right model."[16] Reality, however, proved something very different. Internet businesses didn't get it right the first time. And, in total, they wasted billions trying to attract customers to services and products their intended customers weren't willing to purchase.

Had these e-business pioneers realized that business is always an iterative process of learning from interacting with paying customers, they would have avoided a "bet-the-ranch" approach to attracting customers and would have spent more on developing

As we write this, theglobe.com is trading at less than $1 per share and still searching for that "pathway to profitability" that has replaced get rich.com as the prevailing mindset.

The most optimistic of prospects for a company in this new industry of the Internet was clearly the driver of value, not business fundamentals. Analysts were encouraging investors to throw conservatism out the window and worry about losing upside potential, not about losing the investment.[13]

Truth is, the general public kept being told we were in a new economy, building new industries that would eat the lunch of old economy companies and make us all fabulously wealthy. So maybe the crazy valuations of Internet stocks weren't unreasonable. Maybe a 22-year-old should get millions to start a Web-based business. But deep down inside, we knew. We knew that despite all the innovation taking place at what was reported to be "Internet speed," the basics of business—revenues and profits—had to be generated. Like every gold rush, at some point reality sets in and investors expect a return on their investment. Mines have to produce gold. Businesses have to produce profits. And profits require e-businesses, like any other business, to focus on satisfying customers' changing needs and wants.

The 1999 holiday season drove home the realization that, by and large, Internet companies were not able to satisfy their customers—even unprofitably. The media that track e-commerce painted a picture of a customer experience that was very different from the one the billions of dollars spent on advertising promised. For example, ZDNet reported a litany of e-tail horrors, including "out of stock shock . . . shady delivery claims . . . so-so customer service." And Andersen Consulting reported that "top Web sites crashed, could not take orders, were under construction, had entry blocked, or were otherwise inaccessible."[14]

Whether on Main Street or Cyber Street, building a business is never easy. The vast promise of Web City allowed entrepreneurs to get away with not building profitable operating businesses for a time. But a business that abides in Web City is a business like

had changed. Forever. Again, no major geopolitical events and wars. But on that day, the tech-heavy Nasdaq lost more than trillion in market capitalization in 6.5 hours.[15] No matter spin, the first cycle of the networked economy was over.

Much has been written analyzing investors' flight from te nology stocks. But this book is not about investing in the st market. It's about building profitable companies in the netwo economy. Thus, when we look at the end of the dot-com era ask, "What have we learned?" we are trying to understand w and how the critical assumptions made by entrepreneurs a building businesses in the age of knowledgeable and empow consumers went wrong.

What Have We Learned?

We believe that a critical mistake entrepreneurs and inv made during the early years of the Internet (and that son still making) is that the initial business models that populat Internet were based on a level of understanding of the world simply being transferred to a new medium, the world. In other words, the assumptions used to build these businesses were developed before there was enough time fo entrepreneurs to acquire an understanding of how the Inte

as well as other enabling technologies—is changing basic busine structures.

The Four Building Blocks of Business

Let's look at key assumptions made by the entrepreneurs and investors of the first cycle of the networked economy and see how these assumptions affected what we call the four building blocks of business: process, customers, information, and timing.

an understanding of how best to profitably deliver the solution to their real customers' current set of needs and wants.

Of course, if you have determined in advance that you have the right business model, then it makes sense to spend and spend to attract more and more customers. But if you don't know how to profitably satisfy the first customer, never mind the thousandth customer, it makes very little sense. And how do you know in advance? You can't. You have to try, learn, refine. In short, iterate.

> To be successful you have to try, learn, refine. In short, iterate.

And speaking of rushing to market, another assumption made— one that often accompanies technological innovations—was that to get the glory and the profits, you must be first. Anything else makes you an "also ran." But history is littered with the carcasses of first movers—just consider Sony's Betamax or Apple's Newton. Remember, pioneers often die with arrows in their backs.

Customers. For companies, the Internet promised to provide reams of data through which they could develop more accurate marketing profiles and thereby sell their customers lots of goods and services. For customers, the Internet promised the ability to have their needs and wants satisfied on a personal basis. This face-off worked to the detriment of the companies. It's of no value to a company to consider large marketing blocks as a single entity when, ultimately, consumers want their products and services personalized and sold to them on an individual basis.

It is an odd paradox but true: Although the Internet and the Web involve individuals interacting with a machine, for the individuals it is as if they are interacting one-on-one with the entire company. And the person expects that company to respond with personalized products at the price each individual is willing to pay. If the exact product is not offered or is not offered at the right price, the customer simply clicks on to the next site. If all you are offering on the Web is a mass-produced product, the consumer's prevailing quest is to seek the lowest price, knowing that a better deal is only a click away.

Many e-commerce Web sites still do not go beyond offering mass-produced products at hoped-for low prices. And certainly in the early days of the Web, it was an almost universal belief: *eyeballs = customers = profits.* It was thought that all a dot-com company had to do was attract lots of people (eyeballs) to its Web site. Once at the site, the eyeballs would be so enamored of the company's product or service, they would become loyal customers and these lasting relationships would result in profits. Consequently, metrics such as hits, page views, and unique visitors replaced revenues and profits as indicators of success.

However, rather than *eyeballs = customers = profits,* the truth was *eyeballs = transactions = losses.* But because Internet entrepreneurs and their investors believed that *eyeballs = customers = profits,* between 1995 and 2000, they were willing to spend an average of $82 of their venture capital and IPO money to get each *transaction.* To put that figure into perspective, according to a widely quoted Boston Consulting Group study, catalog companies spend only $11 to acquire a customer, whereas retail stores spend $31.[17] As if those inflated customer acquisition costs weren't bad enough, the focus on bargains and low prices caused many dot-coms to lose money on nearly every sale.

Information. The more you know about your customers and their needs and wants, the easier it is to satisfy them. In the Internet era, however, the belief has grown that it is possible for companies to saw the value chain in half and create two viable sets of relationships: business-to-business (B2B) and business-to-consumer (B2C). Even more surprising is the belief that these two segments can operate successfully independent of one another.

The reasoning is that the Internet facilitates the breakup of the distribution channel and that efficiencies resulting from this division will empower the consumer while enabling the business. Unfortunately, this reasoning is wrong. The main result of artificially segmenting the value chain is that the voice of the consumer is completely left out of the equation because by making a horizontal cut across a vertical pipeline, the flow of information is cut. Businesses on the B2B side of the value chain lose contact with the consumer, and businesses on the B2C side lose contact with the raw materials and the manufacturing.

Information is the lifeblood of business. Whenever the flow of information is restricted, the ability of consumers to get what they want suffers, as does the ability of businesses to operate profitably.

> Information is the lifeblood of business. Whenever the flow of information is restricted, the ability of consumers to get what they want suffers, as does the ability of businesses to operate profitably.

Timing. Internet speed may not be quite as fast as was previously believed. Some Internet companies may have successfully gone public with little revenue, heavy losses, and at a very young age, but that doesn't mean they had viable businesses. Forrester Research's CEO George Colony rightly noted, "Successful companies like Microsoft and Cisco don't get built overnight. They take years of blood, sweat, tears, developed wisdom, and enlightened business decisions."[18]

Businesses can grow up quickly on the Web, but the conventional wisdom misses an extremely important point in the development of any business: The assumptions we make and on which we start and grow a business—whether an e-business or not—are just that: *assumptions*. Leaving aside the physical constraints of establishing a business (i.e., raising money, training employees, etc.), narrowing the margin of error between our assumptions and reality is the length of time it takes to establish a profitable business. And because no one makes perfect assumptions, it always takes time to establish a profitable business.

Narrowing the margin of error between our assumptions and reality is the length of time it takes to establish a profitable business.

So a few folks became very wealthy during the first cycle of the networked economy, but most were left with dashed dreams. The fact that the assumptions about business models that embraced online technologies between August 9, 1995, and April 14, 2000, were not correct should not surprise. They were old assumptions made for old-style business models and, in fact, were not even very good assumptions for old-style business models. On the Internet, it just took less time to see how wrong they were.

Which leaves us with the question, What are the assumptions that should now be operationalized to build a profitable business that embraces a knowledgeable and powerful consumer?

To Reiterate . . .

1. The Netscape stock offering caused a paradigm shift in the public equity markets. A company without profits had successfully offered its shares to the public.

2. During the final half of the 1990s, a healthy market for initial public offerings (IPOs) fueled the work of innovators who were reshaping old-line industries and even creating what was believed to be a new industry, the Internet.

3. The retirement savings of Americans were providing the capital to fuel the development of companies that were in very early stages of growth and without proven business models.

4. The most optimistic of prospects for a company in this new industry of the Internet was clearly the driver of value, not business fundamentals.

5. A critical mistake that entrepreneurs and investors made during the early years of the Internet (and that some are still making) is that the initial business models that populated the Internet were based on a level of understanding of the offline world simply being transferred to a new medium, the online world.

6. The four building blocks of business are process, customers, information, and timing.

7. To be successful you have to try, learn, refine. In short, iterate.

8. If all you are offering on the Web is a mass-produced product, the consumer's prevailing quest is to seek the lowest price, knowing that a better deal is only a click away.

9. Information is the lifeblood of business. Whenever the flow of information is restricted, the ability of consumers to get what they want suffers, as does the ability of businesses to operate profitably.

10. Narrowing the margin of error between our assumptions and reality is the length of time it takes to establish a profitable business.

ENDNOTES

1. Beppi Crosariol, "Netscape IPO Booted Up Debut of Hot Stock Stuns Wall Street Veterans," *Boston Globe,* 10 August 1995, 37.

2. Ibid.

3. A full listing of IPOs in 1995 can be found at <www.iporesources.org/ipolist/ipolist95.html>.

4. Netscape Communications Corporation Condensed Consolidated Statements of Operations (unaudited) for the Three Months Ended June 30, 1995, as reported in Form 10-Q for the Period Ended June 30, 1996; <www.sec.gov/Archives/edgar/data/944458/0000891618-96-001834.txt>.

5. Crosariol, 37.

6. Ibid.

7. Ibid.

8. Jeff Glasser, "Investors Eager to Cash In on Internet Companies," *Boston Globe,* 21 August 1995, 18.

9. A Ponzi scheme, named after Charles Ponzi, who defrauded people in the 1920s, involves getting people to invest in something for a guaranteed rate of return and using the money of later investors to pay off the earlier ones. Who will make money from such a scheme? Those who start it and those who get in early.

10. Kim Cross, McKinsey & Company, "Online Customer Acquisition Costs," *Business 2.0,* November 1999, 316.

11. James Lardner and Paul Sloan, "The Anatomy of Sickly IPOs," *U.S. News & World Report,* 29 May 2000, 42.

12. Greg Ip, et al., "The Internet Bubble Broke Records, Rules, and Bank Accounts," *Wall Street Journal,* 14 July 2000, A1.

13. E. S. Browning and Greg Ip, "Here Are Six Myths That Drove the Boom in Technology Stocks," *Wall Street Journal,* 16 October 2000, A14.

14. Andrea Orr, "One Quarter of Online Purchases Fail," *ZDNet News,* 20 December 1999; <www.zdnet.com/zdnn/stories/news/0,4586,2411982,00.html>.

15. John Ellis, "Digital Matters," *Fast Company,* August 2000, 234.

16. Connie Guglielmo, "Can Webvan Deliver the Goods?" *ZDNet,* 3 February 2000; <dailynews.yahoo.com/h/zd/20000203/tc/20000204109.html>.

17. Shop.org/TheBoston Consulting Group, "The State of Online Retailing 3.0," April 2000; <www.shop.org/nr/00/041700.html>.

18. Fred Vogelstein and Janet Rae-Dupree, "Easy Dot Com, Easy Dot Go," *U.S. News Online,* 1 May 2000; <www.usnews.com/usnews/issue/000501/tech.htm>.

PART TWO

The New Reality

Sir Francis Bacon was right . . . *Knowledge is Power!* Consequently, one of the most profound implications of the rapid shift to the networked economy is the unparalleled access to knowledge everyone now has. As a result, consumers really do have the power. And this changes everything.

Personalization of Goods, Services, and Information

4

The problem with the transformation in the role consumers now play in value creation is that businesses have yet to understand what it really means to dance with a knowledgeable and powerful consumer—a dance in which the consumer leads. And while companies have adopted a more customercentric orientation in their marketing and sales initiatives and have invested millions in customer relationship management (CRM) software applications, by and large the business community still views customers as targets rather than active partners in creating value. Just listen to how CRM is often described: "CRM is a data-oriented strategy that depends on the ability to capture, analyze, and execute against customer profiles."[1] Clearly, when you "execute against customer profiles," you are *targeting* because the customer is viewed as the recipient of the initiative, not as an active participant in the process.

As C. K. Prahalad, Harvey C. Fruehauf Professor of Business Administration at the University of Michigan Business School, along with his coauthors states:

> Traditionally, . . . consumers were passive "target markets" for consumption. Current IT implementation of customer-relationship-management extends this notion from predetermined segments to individual consumers. This is akin to a hunter with binoculars trying to get a better view of the

prey—the targeted consumer. This "game" is rapidly changing. The hunter can become the hunted if companies don't recognize the dramatic transformation of the role of consumers. Consumers are no longer a predetermined category with a specific role of consumption in the industrial system. They are active players in co-creating value.[2]

THE CUSTOMER'S NEW ROLE

It is of vital importance that businesses understand the new role consumers play and encourage their collaboration not only in defining the channels of communication, product testing, and problem solving, but also in the personalization of product and solution development. The dictionary defines *collaboration* as "working

> Businesses must encourage consumers' collaboration in defining the channels of communication, product testing, problem solving, and also in the personalization of product and solution development.

jointly with others or cooperating with an agency or instrumentality with which one is not immediately connected." Consequently, the notion that the consumer collaborates in product development creates a very different definition of personalization than that envisioned by marketers. Marketing messages made personal by the data acrobatics advanced CRM software makes possible, are not the personalization of goods and services as we refer to it.

As we said, the second cycle of the networked economy is increasingly defined by the choices individual consumers want businesses to make available to them, not what a business chooses to make available. *Consumers are increasingly expecting personalized goods, services, and information.*

Today's powerful and knowledgeable consumer no longer accepts mass-marketed offerings and will increasingly become dissatisfied with mass-customized products as technological developments make available more and more personalized solutions. Again, C. K. Prahalad comments: "Although this is a stretch for most companies, in the future successful companies will be those centered on personalized experiences. Progressive companies, whether traditional or Internet-based, recognize this fundamental fact. This means no two individuals may have an identical experience, even if they get an identical bundle of physical products."[3]

And it's not just the individual consumer who wants personalization. "Without a doubt, businesses, like consumers, are demanding greater degrees of personalization."[4]

Let's look at a few examples of the inroads personalization is making in the provision of goods and services. The development of personalized financial Web sites is already growing quickly:

> Benjamin Patch . . . the 29-year-old employee of a software company is one of a small but growing number of people logging on each morning to a personal Web site for an up-to-the-minute tally of their net worth: assets, liabilities, and even airline mileage awards.
>
> This is different from the customized pages of news, e-mail, and advertising cobbled together by Internet service providers. Mr. Patch's personal site shows volumes of sensitive and private financial information, access to which only he can authorize. The speed and scope of the service is impressive.[5]

And then there's Customatix.com, a fledging sports apparel company that just might represent the future of e-tailing:

> The Santa Cruz, Calif.–based company allows footwear fans to design their own sneakers, choosing their own colors, symbols, and fabrics. The blueprint is transmitted to the company's factory in China, and the shoes are shipped within

two weeks. Want pink-and-green running shoes with silver laces? There's no filter for taste.

The carriage trade has always had its custom goods— $3,000 Saville Row suits or a $30,000 custom perfume concoction from the House of Creed. With the help of the Internet, where Dell Computer advanced the cause, personalized goods can be made affordable for the masses.

Nike sells customized sneakers for $50 to $100 a pair. Mattel sells customized Barbie dolls for $40. Procter & Gamble will soon let coffee fans blend their own java.

Like Nike, Customatix.com lets armchair designers create their sneakers, which appear instantly on a 3-D image on the screen. Both companies also allow customers to personalize foot fare with their own slogan.[6]

<www.customatix.com>

Across the board, companies are figuring out how to personalize their offerings. Listen to how Capital One, one of the fastest growing and most profitable businesses in the credit card industry, has introduced personalization:

In 1999, Cap One ran 36,000 product tests. Throughout the process, it sifts and resifts the response data to drill down to the best microsegmentation opportunities.

The cycle of design-test-segment, repeated over and over, allows Cap One to slice a huge customer base into precise and tiny segments. Today, Cap One has more than 27 million customers, no two handled exactly alike. Cap One offers a unique and almost endless array of personalized credit card deals.[7]

And while it may take some time before Ford can build *your* personalized dream car, entrepreneurial companies are already driving down the road to personalization:

Enter Model E Corp., which bills itself as the first Internet build-to-order automobile company. Model E, based in Fremont, California, has a new proposition: The future of the auto industry is building your own car over the Net. Model E thinks that your car should be *your* car, built one mouse click at a time to your exact specifications.

Model E also thinks that the customer experience should be seamless, so the first thing it does is handle all of the time intensive stuff for you. *All of it.* You just go to its Web site, choose from a portfolio of premium automobiles (from such brand name manufacturers as Audi and BMW), add the features you want, and Model E takes care of the rest. The car will be delivered to your home a few days later already inspected, plated, insured, full of gas, and good to go.

. . . The only thing that you have to do is pay the monthly fee for the whole package: the car itself, financing, insurance, and service.[8]

<www.modele.com>

THE REQUIREMENTS OF PERSONALIZATION

Obviously, the shift to personalization hasn't taken hold in every industry. But it will. Lately, not a day goes by that we don't read about a new ability to personalize some group of goods or services. But before we get into the specific implications of how this new requirement for personalization affects your business, it is again worth stressing that the 20th century was about the formation of mass markets and mastering the techniques to cater to them. The 21st century, on the other hand, is increasingly about customers expecting the satisfaction of their needs and wants on a personal basis. Barnes&Noble.com clearly understands this distinction: "At the end of the day, Barnes&Noble.com officials acknowledge that personalization is not a tool to manage customers. Customers empowered by personalization cannot be managed; they can only be served."[9]

To get a personalized solution, however, customers must be prepared to share their personal information. Oh sure, we've had to share our personal information in the offline world in the old economy. To get a bank loan. To get a credit card. To buy health insurance. But it was the exception rather than the rule and it was done for significant products and services. In the world of personalization, to buy a newspaper or a music CD, you will have to share personal information because the newspaper and the CD are modified to subject matter you want to read about and listen to.

As the delivery of personalized goods and services on the part of the business and the purchase of the goods and services on the part of the customer raise many new issues, let's look more closely at what is required by customers and businesses to actually satisfy *personal* needs and wants:

Customer Requirements

1. The degree of importance to the customer that a particular set of needs and wants is satisfied personally
2. The degree of time and effort that the customer must put into providing personal information
3. The willingness of the customer to change behavior
4. The willingness of the customer to share personal information

Business Requirements

1. The development of and adherence to privacy policies

2. The degree of personalization required by the product and/or service
3. The presence of the business infrastructure to actually provide the personalization
4. The company's ability to operate profitably

For example, if a consumer wants to receive personalized news, he or she must take the time to inform the news provider what type of news is of interest. A similar investment in time, effort, and information is needed to supply data on tastes in music, movies, clothes, and the like. As you can see, in order for customers to receive personalized goods and services they *must* be willing to share their time and energy with the businesses providing the solution. Consumers have to decide whether the benefit of having their needs and wants personally satisfied is worth the required time and effort and any possible discomfort resulting from revealing personal information. So, essentially, the consumer does a cost-benefit analysis as part of the decision process. And the time and effort involved in the personalization of goods and services are not always as simple as filling out a form.

Look at how apparel cataloger Lands' End's Web site describes what it is doing:

Body Scanning takes the guesswork out of sizing—and puts the fun in—by creating an online image of you using today's most advanced technology.

When you visit our Body Scanning Truck, now touring selected cities, you step into a scanning room to the tune of upbeat music. In seconds, bursts of white light have recorded 200,000 points of measuring data—enough to determine your size and dimensions more accurately than ever.

Once you're scanned, you're ready to experience the new My Virtual Model™. Created from your personal body scan, it's the most realistic, size-accurate virtual model anywhere. Use it to try on clothes, create outfits, be surer than ever what size you should buy.

Body Scanning—measuring accuracy at the speed of light
Gives you your exact dimensions
- Recommends which Lands' End size to buy
- Only at landsend.com

Sounds like science fiction, doesn't it? But Body Scanning is simply a brand new technology available to the consumer. It's fast, easy, safe, and fun—and more accurate than tape measures ever dreamed of.

The entire experience takes about 10 minutes, including about 15 seconds in the Image Twin™ scanner. When you're done, you'll have a printout with accurate measurements, as well as a log-in ID and password for accessing My Virtual Model™ online. A couple of hours later, your size accurate model will be ready for you to use, and go shopping with.

Never before has body scanning been used with virtual modeling. It's a whole new technology dedicated to making your online shopping easier and better. But it's only a beginning, and perhaps a humble one. This fall's tour provides an introduction to body scanning.[10]

Although some people may think it's fun to have a computer take pictures of them standing in the skintight underwear they have to put on, a number of folks will undoubtedly feel it isn't worth the effort, never mind the concern about what Lands' End might do with the computer images of them in their underwear. So implicitly what consumers will do is evaluate the effort required on their part associated with what Lands' End asks them to do— go where the truck is situated, wait in line, change into the special underwear, pose for the computer scanner, wait to make sure the images are usable, and so on—against the benefit of having a virtual image of how they'll look in any of the items Lands' End has available. And while we, as customers, only have to do this once as long as our body dimensions don't change much, the gain realized—seeing how we'll look in their clothes—has to exceed the energy and time required; otherwise, we consumers will not opt-in to the process in the first place.

And it's not just the time and energy involved. It's changes in buying habits and/or patterns. Any change in behavior required of a consumer to get a personal solution will cause the consumer to consider the cost of changing behavior against the benefit of receiving a personal solution. Companies therefore need to understand what degree of benefit is required to motivate a behavioral change by the consumer. For example, it was assumed when consumers began to use the Web for shopping that they would also use the online customer service and support (e.g., e-mail and frequently asked questions). That assumption was wrong. Companies quickly realized that consumers still wanted to have a personal conversation with them. In other words, consumers were *not* willing to change their behavior.

Even when a small change in behavior is requested, it still requires a large benefit for consumers to go along. Priceline.com has asked consumers to change the way they buy in order to get the best price possible on airline tickets. This works only for the small number of people for whom price is the most important factor in their personal travel decisions:

> [Gartner Group analyst Rob] Labatt notes that consumers who use Priceline.com's core airline ticket buying service must agree to make their purchase before they find out exactly which flight they are on or which airports they might have to use. Consumers also have to be aware of current competitive prices in order to haggle for the best possible deal, he says.
>
> "It takes quite a lot of research to even know what price to bid," Labatt adds. "That's a lot of work for a savings that can often be quite small.
>
> "I've heard, just anecdotally, from a lot of people who tried the service and who ended up getting tickets to places they really didn't want to go at times they really didn't want to travel," Labatt says. "Those people use it once, but they don't use it again."[11]

BUILDING TRUST

Our fourth customer requirement for personalized solutions is the willingness to share personal information. From the point of view of the company, we might wonder why consumers wouldn't be willing to share their personal information so that our business could use that information to provide the desired personal solution? Many factors enter into the decision process, but at the end of the day from the point of view of the consumer, it really boils down to a question of trust: *Can I trust the company to protect my personal information?*

In one sense, it really is that simple. No trust. No personal information. No personal satisfaction.

> It really is simple. No trust. No personal information. No personal satisfaction.

Unfortunately, in another sense, it's more complicated. If we can't resolve the issue of trust, consumers will not provide companies with their personal information and thus the whole flow of value creation toward personalization will be held up, not by a lack in technology but, quite frankly, by a failure in human character to establish the level of trust needed for business in the 21st century. Speaking to this point, Bill Gates believes "that if we do privacy right, users will see that having information about themselves subject to certain principles is very helpful. When you leave a store, you won't say, 'Hey, if I ever come back in here, don't recognize me and don't remember what I bought before. Just forget I was ever here.'"[12]

Of course, there's no getting around the fact that it takes time to build trust. How long it takes depends on the specific situation, but clearly it's not automatic, nor is it realistic to expect that it can be built overnight. Nor are issues of trust exclusive to the

Internet. They've always been present in the offline world as well. However, what is different is the level of trust we now need and the vast number of people we have to trust.

How do we make it work? Businesspeople need to be aware of the new level of trust that is required. In the Industrial Age, trust was about contracts between businesses and customers and between businesses and other businesses. Contracts basically stated that in exchange for a certain sum of money provided by Y, X will sell a certain good or service. But in the age of the personalization of goods and services, the contract and the level of trust is expanded. Contracts now state that in exchange for a certain sum of money *and information* provided by Y, X will sell a certain personalized good or service; but implicit or explicit in that contract must be the understanding that personal information will not be abused. Otherwise, the flow of personal information will cease and commerce will have to regress to the age when everyone had to make do rather than rise to the more fulfilling level of personalization where everyone buys exactly what he or she needs and wants.

In fact, concern about trust and privacy on the Internet has prompted the birth of dozens of codes and legislative proposals to ensure the confidence of the consumer. Here is an example of the Better Business Bureau's Net Conduct Code:

> In an effort to promote public trust in Internet transactions, the Better Business Bureau (BBB) and BBBOnLine unveiled the BBB Code of Online Business Practices.
>
> According to the BBB, the code is designed to guide ethical business-to-consumer conduct in domestic and international e-commerce transactions, and is already being used as a model in Europe and elsewhere.
>
> "The Code provides standards that, when adopted by online merchants and advertisers, are expected to make a significant contribution toward effective self-regulation in the public interest," said Calvin J. Collier, chair of the Council of Better Business Bureaus.

. . . The code of conduct has the support of both the U.S. Federal Trade Commission and the European Union.

The BBB Code of Online Business Practices is based on five principles:

- **Truthful and Accurate Communications.** The code says that online advertisers should not engage in any deceptive or misleading behavior in the use of advertising, marketing, or technology.
- **Disclosure.** Under the code, online merchants are to disclose to their current and prospective customers relevant information about their business, products offered for sale, and the transaction.
- **Information Practices and Security.** The code says that online advertisers should adopt practices that treat consumers' information with care, post and adhere to a fair privacy policy, and respect consumers' preferences regarding unsolicited e-mail.
- **Customer Satisfaction.** The code also encourages e-tailers to work to ensure that customers are satisfied by taking steps to honor promises made to consumers, answering questions, and working to resolve complaints in a timely and responsive manner.
- **Protecting Children.** The code says that online advertisers who target children under the age of 13 should take "special care to protect them" by recognizing their developing cognitive abilities.[13]

<www.bbbonline.com/code/code.asp>

Although codes and legislation may help, individual companies are responsible for their own relationship with their customers. And just as in the offline world where some companies earn the trust of their customers and others do not, the same situation exists in the online world. As in the old John Houseman ad for Smith Barney, "They make money the old-fashioned way. They earn it." Trust can only be built the old-fashioned way. It has to be earned. And the way to earn the trust of customers offline or online is to treat them honestly and with respect. Corny but nonetheless true. And that means honesty and respect not just as part of your ad campaign or your mission statement but in actual fact. Companies with excellent products and excellent service earn the trust of their customers. However, earning the trust of your customers is not in itself enough. WordPerfect was an excellent company with an excellent product that had earned the trust of its customers, but it failed to add a timely Windows-based version and thus lost almost all of its market share to Microsoft. Still, when it was a product customers wanted, trust was a key element to WordPerfect's success.

In the age of personalization, trust assumes an even more important role because it is a necessary prerequisite for personalization. We can be cynical (because in the previous paragraph we were very old-fashioned), and contend that most businesses won't have the character to rise to that level of trust, but, interestingly enough, we can be even more cynical and contend that they will. Why? Because the personalization of goods and services holds out the promise of creating a vast amount of wealth, and that wealth will not be established unless and until sufficient trust is established; and, let's face it, money is a very good motivator. Trust us on that.

Over time, successful companies will build the level of trust required by the consumer to allow the required behavior change and the sharing of personal information. Building a relationship with your customers is like building every other relationship. It's done in steps and it takes time. Confidence grows as each party fulfills its contractual obligations. We must remember the consumer needs to see a strong benefit to justify putting in the effort required. However, once you gain the trust of consumers and they provide you with their personal information, they're yours to lose.

Now that we have a better understanding of the issues customers take into consideration, we can turn our attention to the factors that are important to a business involved in providing personalized goods and services.

As we've seen, companies need to develop and implement explicit policies for using their customers' personal information. These policies need to exist in both word and deed and be straightforward, uncomplicated, and monitored for adherence by *all* employees.

Companies need to identify the actual level of personalization that is required by a specific product and service. For example, the level of personalization may require nothing more than, like Amazon, aggregating a selection of goods desired by the customer, or it may require a greater level of personalization such as cutting and stitching jeans to each customer's specific measurements like Levi Strauss.

The company then needs to create the business infrastructure required to actually undertake the personalization. For example, we saw that Customatix.com links to a factory in China as part of its infrastructure to produce personalized sneakers. And, of course, the company then needs to make sure that it can make an acceptable *profit* with that business model. (In Part Three we discuss these issues in greater detail.)

Of vital importance is that businesses understand the new role consumers play and encourage their collaboration, not only in defining the channels of communication, product testing, and problem solving, but also in developing personalized products and solutions. While technology is enabling companies to respond to consumers' personal needs and wants, it is incumbent on companies to recognize that at the start of the second cycle of the networked economy, we're at the point where consumers are now leading the dance.

To Reiterate . . .

1. The problem with the transformation in the role consumers now play in value creation is that businesses have yet to understand and appreciate what it really means to dance with a knowledgeable and powerful consumer—a dance in which the consumer leads.

2. The notion that the consumer is involved in product development creates a very different definition of personalization than that envisioned by marketers.

3. In order for customers to receive personalized goods and services, they *must* be willing to share their time and energy with the businesses providing the solution. Consumers have to decide whether the benefit of having their needs and wants personally satisfied is worth the required time and effort, and revealing personal information.

4. Any change in behavior required of a consumer to get a personalized solution will cause the consumer to consider the cost of changing behavior against the benefit of receiving a personalized solution.

5. If we can't resolve the issue of trust, consumers will not provide companies with their personal information, and thus the whole flow of value creation toward personalization will be held up, not by a lack in technology, but, quite frankly, by a failure in human character to establish the level of trust needed for business in the 21st century.

6. Trust can only be built the old-fashioned way. It has to be earned. And the way to earn the trust of custom-

ers offline or online is to treat them honestly and with respect.

7. A company needs to create the business infrastructure required to actually undertake personalization.

8. Of vital importance is that businesses understand the new role consumers play and encourage their collaboration, not only in defining the channels of communication, product testing, and problem solving, but also in developing personalized products and solutions.

ENDNOTES

1. Scott Nelson, "Privacy Storm Clouds Gather," *Executive Edge,* October/November 2000, 19.

2. Reprinted with permission of *Information Week,* CMP Media, Manhasset, NY. C. K. Prahalad, Venkatram Ramaswamy, and M.S. Krishnan, "Consumer Centricity," *Informationweek Online,* 10 April 2000; <www.informationweek.com/781/prahalad>.

3. Ibid.

4. Bob Kramich, of NECX.com, quoted by Bernie Libster, "Can B2B Marketers Personalize?" *1 to 1 Personalization,* October/November 2000, 16.

5. Jathon Sapsford, "Personalized Financial Web Sites Spread, Amid Privacy Concerns," *Wall Street Journal,* 19 July 2000, C1. Reprinted by permission of the publisher via Copyright Clearance Center, Inc.

6. Krysten A. Crawford, "Customizing for the Masses," *Forbes,* 16 October 2000, 168. Reprinted by permission of Forbes Magazine © 2000 Forbes.

7. Adrian Slywotzky and David Morrison, "Off the Grid," *The Industry Standard,* 23 October 2000, 205.

8. John Ellis, "The Future of the Auto Industry Is Building Your Own Car Over the Net," *Fast Company,* December 2000, 330.

9. John Kador, "Delivering Long-Term Value," *1 to 1 Personalization,* October/November 2000, 52.

10. © Lands' End, Inc. Used with permission; <www.landsend.com/ spawn.cgi?target=SCANTOUR1000&sid=0972338953559>.

11. Hal Plotkin, "Priceline Business Model Seen Flawed," cnbc.com, 3 October 2000; <www.cnbc.com/commentary/commentary_full_ story_stocks.asp?StoryID=24016>.

12. Bill Gates, "A Future as Big as Your In-box," *Business 2.0,* 26 September 2000, 134.

13. Lori Enos, "Consumer Watchdog Unveils Net Conduct Code," 25 October 2000. Reprinted with permission of *E-Commerce Times,* part of the NewsFactor Network; <www.ecommercetimes.com/news/ articles2000/001025-1.shtml>.

5

Shared Interests

U_p to this point, we have presented our belief that because
of advances in information and communication technologies, the
balance of power between consumers and businesses now favors
knowledgeable and empowered consumers who require the satisfaction of their needs and wants on a personal basis. In the last
chapter, we saw that while the personalization of goods and services holds the promise of creating a vast amount of wealth, that
wealth will not be realized unless and until sufficient trust is established between customers and the companies with which they
do business. In this chapter we show how the shift in power to
consumers changes the dynamics of the relationship between customers and businesses. Specifically, we intend to show how that
shift requires companies to look at their relationship with customers from the customers' perspective. It's all about what customers need and want, not their profile and not what businesses
need and want.

> Companies need to look at their relationship with
> customers from each customer's perspective.

THE POWER SHIFTS

When we think about industries today, we think about the movie industry, the clothing industry, the automobile industry, the oil industry, and so on, thus we think of them in a product or service orientation. What they do and how they do it. That orientation tends to define companies from the business's perspective rather than the customer's.

It's our view, however, that in the 21st century, because of the shift in the balance of power between consumers and businesses, looking at companies from the perspective of the business no longer makes sense. Given the changed marketplace, it is of greater benefit to think about companies from the customer's viewpoint. And from a customer's perspective, it's never about what industry you're in or what products you make. It's only about the satisfaction of personal needs and wants.

Think again of Henry Ford. If all his customers were satisfied with black Model Ts, Ford didn't have to spend much time focusing on his customers and discovering what their exact set of needs and wants were. He had to focus on his business. If he turned out well-made cars inexpensively, he knew more than enough customers would buy his cars. On the other hand, as customers became more selective and desired cars in different colors, Ford had to spend much more time focusing on his customers. If they were picky about color, they'd be picky about other items. And as Ford was in competition with other car manufacturers, he had to focus on his customers even more. The more the customer demands, the more the business is obligated to focus on the customer.

Unfortunately, it's always simpler and therefore more tempting to focus on the business. Solving production problems or employee satisfaction problems, as tough as they may be, are easier to deal with because you have more control. You can change the assembly line, buy newer and better technology, change work hours, and so on. Customers, whether individuals or other businesses, present greater difficulties because you have less control. There are always more unknown factors. Needs and wants change. The price customers will pay changes. Tastes change. And customers always have the ultimate power to buy somewhere else.

As we saw in Chapter 2, in the age of mass production, products were designed to suit millions of people and companies looked at customers on the basis of market profiles. When making products for large numbers of people, market profiles of large market segments were the tool of choice because individual variations were not necessary or technologically feasible. As manufacturing improved and variety became more important, mass production evolved into mass customization. Market segments got smaller, but the numbers were still large enough so that profiles worked. Even today, as we move into the age of personalization, customer profiles are still used. They're ingrained as a marketing tool, and companies have grown comfortable focusing on the customer, based on demographic and psychographic profiling variables. To date, CRM personalization software has not reached the level of true personalization but is based on building profiling tools that slice and dice the reams of clickstream data Web sites collect into ever finer descriptions of customer profiles. And, of course, not all customers always interact with a company via its Web site, thereby rendering these profiles incomplete.

However, the personalization of goods and services—not just the personalization of the marketing message—is rapidly becoming so important that it no longer makes sense to limit the understanding of customers to their profile, no matter how narrowly defined. The variety, the individuality is too significant. In the age of personalization, what assumes primary importance is not who the consumer is in terms of age or income and the like but rather the set of needs and wants that the consumer has. It's not that profiles are totally irrelevant. When you are identifying a set of shared interests, a profile can provide some sense of who is most likely to have that set of needs and wants and whether it's a community broad enough to be worth going after. But, ultimately, the goods and services that your company provides must satisfy customers on an individual basis. So what is of critical importance is not the customer profiles you are trying to sell to but rather the set of customer needs and wants you're trying to satisfy.

> What is of critical importance is not the customer profiles you are trying to sell to but rather the set of customer needs and wants you're trying to satisfy.

This difference between profiles and needs and wants is extremely important. We focus on the set of shared interests rather than the customer profile because by doing so, we are making decisions from the customer's viewpoint and not the company's. As we discussed in Chapter 4, now that the balance of power is shifting to consumers, the interface with business must change too. Customers are now expecting to "sit at the table" and collaborate in the development of the goods, services, and information to satisfy their personal needs and wants, as can be seen in Figure 5.1. And because we are viewing a business from the perspective of the customer's specific desires, it makes it easier for other customers who share those needs and wants to see your business as satisfying them as well.

THE DEFINING SET OF NEEDS AND WANTS

The questions are How do we define a set of needs and wants? and How does focusing on this set of needs and wants make a difference to your business?

As individuals, we all have thousands of needs and wants, ranging from the essentials of life to the latest music recordings. Experience shows we deal with these needs and wants best by grouping them into sets. We think of them in terms of experiences; and, as a result, for companies it therefore makes sense to group its customers' needs and wants into sets related to these same experiences. For example, when purchasing a house, we think of our needs as finding the house, negotiating the deal, arranging the

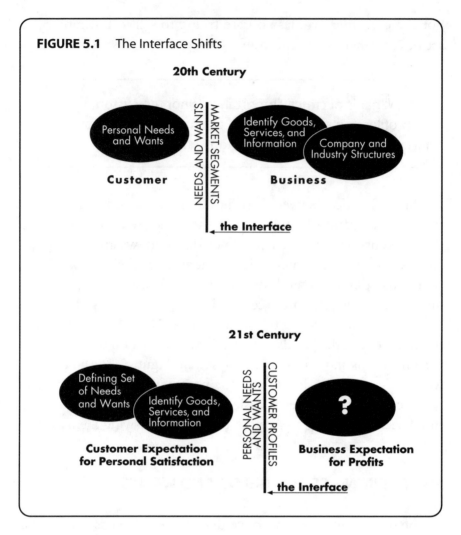

FIGURE 5.1   The Interface Shifts

financing, obtaining insurance, selling our existing house, moving, establishing new utility connections, renovating and remodeling, and so forth. Yet companies tend to divide these same needs and wants into the industries they belong to. In this example, despite the fact that all of the services described are related to the experience of one customer selling one house and occupying another, today the consumer has to engage in relationships with many different businesses in many different industries: real estate, finance, insurance, and so on, to satisfy one buying experience—that is, to satisfy one set of needs and wants.

Therefore, we can see that if we structure a business from the customer's point of view, we get a different business than if we establish a business from the point of view of the business. From the point of view of a set of shared interests, we might have a business that encompasses real estate, finance, moving, storage, decorating, and so on. From the point of view of the business, we get what we have now—different industries providing products and services that customers have to deal with simultaneously or in sequence. The 1-to-1 marketing team of Don Peppers and Martha Rogers offer this prediction: "Consumers will come to regard a handful of companies as their gatekeepers. These gatekeepers will know their customers—values, preferences, interests, and goals—and use the knowledge to increase their 'share of customer.'"[1]

And from Bill Gates: "What the customer really wants is much more aggregated than individual offerings, so how can you create a set of companies to do those aggregations without getting the complexity and the bureaucracy that come from actually putting all those businesses together? The Internet lets you do that."[2]

When you think of yourself as being in the mortgage business, the insurance business, or the real estate business, you may think of the needs and wants of your customers, but it is thinking with blinders on. The blinders restrict your thinking to just the needs and wants of your customers as they relate to the specific industry you are in. But when you forget what industry you're in and just think of the set of needs and wants of your customer, the blinders vanish and you suddenly see your customers in a whole new light: as individuals with a much vaster range of needs and wants—and a much greater wallet to capture.

BUSINESSES ARE ALSO CONSUMERS

It is important to note that throughout this book when we talk of consumers, we mean not only individual end users. *Businesses are consumers too.* And just as companies that deal directly with individual consumers have to recognize these consumers' personalized set of needs and wants, companies that deal only with other businesses have to recognize that these individual businesses also have their own sets of needs and wants. Moreover, if your business deals exclusively with other businesses, you cannot ignore that at the end of the value chain lurks the ultimate consumer. As a business, no matter where you are in the value chain, it is always critical to understand the value proposition the end consumer perceives and then identify how best to provide it. Whether your customer resells your offering, adds to it, or consumes it is, of course, important to the structuring of your business model, but it matters not as you examine the role your company plays in the pipeline between raw materials and the consumption of the finished product. As automobile manufacturers in the 1970s discovered, forcing goods through the value chain only results in a clog in the pipeline unless there is a willing consumer at the other end. And while that example utilizes a physical product, the same logic applies to digitized goods and services.

But that still leaves us with the question of how narrowly or how broadly do we define the set of needs and wants.

THE NEEDS AND WANTS CONTINUUM

Generally speaking, the set of needs and wants has to be narrow enough so that consumers can opt into what becomes a group and yet broad enough so that, from the company's perspective, a profit can be made satisfying all those with that set of needs and wants. The consumer group is best thought of as a self-identifying virtual community that is defined by its set of needs and wants.

> The set of needs and wants has to be narrow enough so that consumers opt in and broad enough so that a profit can be made satisfying all those with that set of needs and wants.

Its members may cover the world or be located in one geographical area. The salient feature of each community is its specific set of needs and wants. The community does not have to literally come together at any time, although that is entirely possible. Nor do they have to know who the other members of the community are. And all the interactions don't have to be Internet-based. The Internet is a communication tool that can facilitate much of the activity of the community—but it is not required that everyone use it.

Some of these communities are so natural and widespread you might already be a member of several dynamic consumer communities based on your interest in such things as adventure travel, baseball, office management, or entrepreneurship. These virtual communities thus represent unprecedented opportunities for companies to gather the information they need to make the products and services to precisely satisfy their customers. Focusing on identifying the set of needs and wants that your business can satisfy most economically (i.e., profitably and at the scale desired) will not reach every individual who has that set of needs and wants. For you as a company, however, the community provides a wealth of information that very closely approximates the complete set of individualized needs and wants—that is, the shared interests of the entire community.

The important point is that the set of needs and wants defines the community as opposed to a profile of who the individuals are (e.g., their age or income or geographical location). As C. K. Prahalad states, "Managers will be forced to explicitly recognize and facilitate the formation and evolution of thematic consumer communities."[3] Prahalad's "thematic consumer communities" are what we see as the consumer community. Again, the individuals that comprise the community are similar because of the shared interests they desire to have satisfied and not because the individuals fit a particular consumer profile.

Let's look at a simple example that is depicted in Figure 5.2. Suppose a local company wants to provide all of the goods and services related to the sports needs of Boston sports fans. The business might see a huge opportunity, but it might not be of

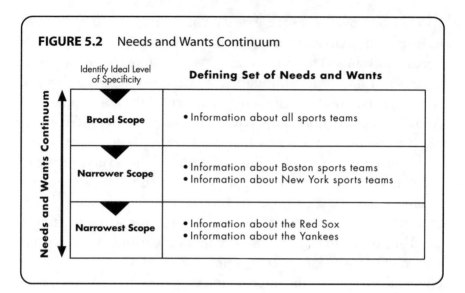

FIGURE 5.2   Needs and Wants Continuum

	Identify Ideal Level of Specificity	Defining Set of Needs and Wants
Broad Scope	▼	• Information about all sports teams
Narrower Scope	▼	• Information about Boston sports teams • Information about New York sports teams
Narrowest Scope	▼	• Information about the Red Sox • Information about the Yankees

interest to you, even though you're a sports fan and live in Boston, because you root for New York teams. But, of course, for a business, there may be little profitability in satisfying the needs and wants of Boston-based New York sports fans. Thus, the challenge is to find the "best" balance between the number of customers who share the set of needs and wants, the ability of the customers to recognize the group as applicable to them, and the business's ability to satisfy those desires profitably.

In the Boston sports example, if we had focused on profiles rather than shared interests, a marketing profile most likely would have targeted males between the ages of 15 and 50 living in Massachusetts, and so on. And while that is useful information for providing a sense of the boundaries of the customers we're going after, it excludes many other potential customers that fall outside the profile. In truth, women, older men, folks living outside the state, for example, might share the same interests. We realize that profiles can change over time as the company gains a better understanding of who really is the customer. But it is our view that by focusing on the set of needs and wants, you get a much better understanding of what you have to do to satisfy your customers on a personal basis.

As we discussed in Chapter 4, the degree of personalization in a given solution/market basket of goods and services is directly related to the willingness of all participants in the value creation process to openly share information. And there is also a cost-benefit analysis that must be applied to every detail, not just from the consumer's perspective of time, effort, and information, but also from the business's perspective of infrastructure and profitability.

Businesses will not offer personalized solutions unless they can do so profitably with the flexibility and at the scale they require for success. And as we've mentioned, it is also important to define a set of needs and wants that is easily recognizable as relevant to the customer. In other words (to keep with our sports business example), if a business is on the Web as BostonSports.com, and we, as a consumer, love all Boston sports, we might stop at that site. However, if our sole passion is the Red Sox, we might not stop at the Boston site because we may not want to bother wading through all the other sports information.

Thus, defining the set of the needs and wants that a business intends to satisfy for its customers is a function of the following:

- The customer's ability to recognize him- or herself as having the set of needs and wants that comprises the consumer community
- The customer's belief that he or she will satisfy his or her individual needs and wants by joining the community and sharing their personal information
- The business's ability to profitably deliver the personalized goods and services the customers require

Let's look at eight specific advantages of focusing on a particular set of needs and wants rather than on consumer profiles:

1. When you focus on a set of needs and wants, you derive better information both about the product and/or service required and about the individual customers for whom you're providing the solution. For example, a friend of ours

recently bought an electric wall heater made by a large manufacturer. As soon as he installed the heater, he realized it wouldn't work because, while the unit heated the room efficiently and economically, at certain speeds it made an irritating high-pitched whine. When he called the manufacturer to complain, he was told it was a new product, and he was put through to the engineer who had designed the heater. When our friend mentioned the noise, the engineer protested that he had tested the heater and it was 25 percent quieter than comparable models. Our friend noted that it wasn't the volume; it was the pitch that was irritating. At that point, the engineer admitted that he had measured the heater's sound level with instruments, but had only used the heater himself in the factory where it was noisy, and thus the pitch had never bothered him. The company took the heater back and returned our friend's money, but the company had created a product that failed to meet the right set of needs and wants. It had not focused on the customer. It had focused on the product. Focusing on the product, it got a working heater, but focusing on the set of needs and wants might have warned the engineer that pitch was as important as volume and that the heaters might be used in quiet environments. This point is not just about product testing; it's about attitude. It's about approach. It's about a way of thinking. Looking at customers from a distance as is done in customer profiles is no longer the way to do business. You have to look at customers as partners. As co-designers. As collaborators. What customers want is key. And if you devote time and money to finding out what the set of needs and wants of your customers are, you simultaneously become better acquainted with your customers. You know who they are because they have helped design the product.

2. Focusing on the set of needs and wants promotes personal communication instead of mass communication. The more you know about your customers, the better you can reach them. We've discussed that marketing profiles provide you

with a spectrum of people wider than those who want your product. By focusing on the set of needs and wants, you discover a narrower range. For example, when we talked about the marketing profile for those who are most likely to be Boston sports fans, we had a range of males from ages 15 to 50. But some in that group are obviously not sports fans and many others outside that group obviously are. Focusing on the set of needs and wants forces you to recognize all the people who have that set of needs and wants, which allows you to know the full range of your customers while at the same time permitting more personal communication, because knowing who your customers are is the key to reaching them. Narrow casting is always more cost effective than "broadcasting." Thus, you might find that small local sports magazines and certain hobby magazines may actually reach more of your potential customers than major city newspapers.

3. Focusing on the set of needs and wants overcomes some of the issues of trust and concerns about abusing personal information we discussed in the previous chapter. For instance, it is common for businesses today to ask customers to provide more information than is necessary for any particular transaction. This tactic derives from the drive for data for marketing profiles and from the belief that a large grab bag of information may potentially help the company "down the road." However, as customers increasingly control access to their personal information, they will be less willing to share such information. For example, a customer might say, "You don't need to know my business's revenue or how many employees I have if I'm simply registering to attend a conference." Focusing on needs and wants instead of profiles helps a company identify and collect only that information necessary for the personalization of goods and services, leaving customers more willing to supply the data and with a greater sense that their privacy will not be infringed. Correctness of focus builds trust.

4. Focusing on the set of needs and wants leads to greater loyalty. Customers who have invested time and effort in defining their set of needs and wants are less likely to fulfill their desires elsewhere. This point, of course, assumes that you have incorporated their input into your product and/or service and that your customers are satisfied.

5. Focusing on the set of needs and wants leads to a greater share of the customer's wallet. Again to take our Boston sports fan example, when you understand the set of shared interests of these customers, you understand better how to capture a greater share of their wallet. For instance, if Harry spends $500 a year on sports-related activities and materials, and he purchases $250 from you, then you have a 50 percent share of Harry's wallet. As it always takes less time and money to increase your share of an existing customer's wallet than to acquire a new customer, you are better off trying to get Harry to spend more money with you. By focusing on Harry's set of needs and wants, you might find a strong interest in sports nostalgia or an interest in a minor league Boston sports team that is more popular than you thought. It's not that you couldn't have discovered these interests in other ways, but it's that business is about time and money. Focusing on the set of needs and wants leads you to this information in less time and for less money.

6. Focusing on the set of needs and wants allows you to capture the customer's enthusiasm. When an individual buys a product, it can be a source of frustration, satisfaction, or enthusiasm. Obviously, a poorly made product or a product that does not fill a customer's needs and wants leads to frustration. A good product produces satisfaction. But a well-made product that does exactly what a customer wants generates enthusiasm. When you are focusing on the set of needs and wants of customers, you are more likely to make products that fill your customers' requirements exactly, and you are thus going to capture more of your customer's enthusiasm. An enthusiastic customer is loyal,

more likely to tell others about your product or service, and more willing to give you the information you need to continue to satisfy his or her needs and wants.

7. Focusing on the set of needs and wants allows you to more easily set up the business model that fulfills the customer's requirements. In the beginning of this book, we quoted Ford's Nasser as asking, "Am I the CEO of a motor company, or am I building wireless, mobile consumer services?" Depending on the answer, Ford can become a radically different company. The answer is really a consequence of the set of the needs and wants of Ford's customers. It doesn't matter that Ford has always been an automotive company. What matters is what Ford's customers expect from Ford today and in the future.

8. Focusing on the set of needs and wants is the only way you can run a profitable business. Business is a dance where the customer leads and the company follows. But as it is a dance, the two must always dance in rhythm. The company must structure itself to follow the customer and quickly change to the customer's rhythm. If you focus on the set of needs and wants of the customer, you'll better feel that rhythm.

To Reiterate . . .

1. Companies need to look at their relationship with customers from customers' perspective. It's all about what customers need and want, not their profile and not what businesses need and want.

2. If we structure a business from the customers' point of view as a set of needs and wants, we get a different business than if we establish a business from the point of view of the business.

3. Throughout this book the word *consumers* doesn't mean only individual end users. Businesses are consumers too.

4. The set of needs and wants has to be narrow enough so that consumers can opt in to what becomes the consumer group and yet broad enough so that, from the company's perspective, a profit can be made satisfying that set of needs and wants.

5. Defining the set of the needs and wants that a business intends to satisfy for its customers is a function of the following:

   • The customer's ability to recognize him- or herself as having the needs and wants that comprise the consumer community
   • The customer's belief that by joining the community and sharing his or her personal information, he or she will satisfy his or her individual needs and wants
   • The business's ability to profitably deliver the personalized goods and services the customers require

6. A company realizes many advantages by focusing on customers' needs and wants rather than on customer profiles.

ENDNOTES

1. Don Peppers and Martha Rogers, "It's a Matter of Time," *Business 2.0,* 26 September 2000, 141.
2. Bill Gates, "A Future as Big as Your In-box."
3. C. K. Prahalad, et al., "Consumer Centricity."

The Entrepreneurial Mindset

6

As we've seen, it is difficult for any one company to deliver the personalized goods and services that satisfy its customers' complete set of needs and wants. As a result, visionary entrepreneurs are developing seamless alliances with the businesses best able to provide their customers with those personalized goods and services. This networking of consumers and businesses holds the potential to create powerful virtual communities of shared interests and vast economic potential that we call *Collaborative Communities*™. Simply put, any business that is involved in the

> The networking of consumers and businesses holds the potential to create powerful virtual communities of shared interests and vast economic potential that we call *Collaborative Communities.*

making and/or delivery of goods and services to the consumer is no longer part of a linear value chain but is part of a broader, more dynamic, interconnected, collaborative community, where each member benefits by focusing on profitably satisfying the personal needs and wants of the consumer group that defines the community. Think of the Collaborative Community as the value creation process for the networked economy.

> Think of the Collaborative Community as the value creation process for the networked economy.

A NEW BUSINESS PATTERN

As shown in Figure 6.1, the Collaborative Community is composed of knowledgeable and powerful consumers, who control the "score" by the selective sharing of the information businesses need to satisfy them one at a time on a personal basis. The totality of any given consumer's set of needs and wants are defined from the consumer's perspective by interest areas or experiences,

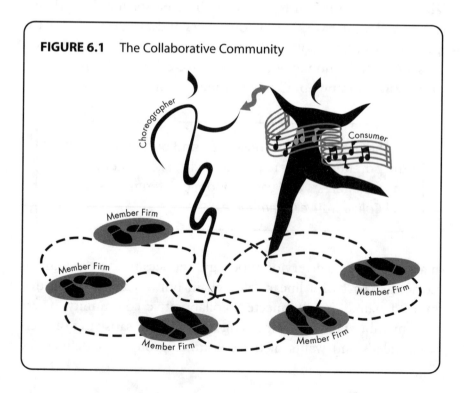

FIGURE 6.1   The Collaborative Community

such as our house-buying or car-buying experience, an interest in Boston sports teams, or how to efficiently manage an office complex. Because Collaborative Communities are organized around a specific set of consumer needs and wants, every consumer is therefore a member of many communities at any given time. And as consumers' needs and wants change over time and consumers develop new sets of needs and wants, the consumer can be thought of as continuously opting into and out of communities. In the same way, businesses are also likely to belong to more than one community at any given time. For example, a manufacturer of canoes, kayaks, and sailboats may belong to a community centered on adventure enthusiasts, and it may belong to another community focused on sailing. And just as consumers opt into and out of communities, businesses opt into and out of communities as consumer needs change and new technologies are developed and introduced. Further, any business will have various networks of companies that it will work with in producing its different product offerings. So we can look at the world as an interlaced, interchanging network of self-identifying communities both on the part of consumers and businesses.

> We can look at the world as an interlaced, interchanging network of self-identifying communities both on the part of consumers and businesses.

Let's take a simple example. Say you are a shoe manufacturer specializing in selling walking shoes through catalogs and the Internet. Your Collaborative Community consists of those companies that supply you with everything you need to make, package, sell, and ship the walking shoes. In addition, because we are talking about eliminating the blinders of legacy thinking and are focusing on your business from the perspective of the customer's entire walking shoe experience from city touring to mountain hiking to camping, your Collaborative Community might also include other outdoor gear manufacturers, camping equipment makers, book publishers, and travel agencies.

But because no one company has the expertise to provide all of these products, the Collaborative Community thus consists of the group of businesses (member firms) that can best satisfy 100 percent of a hiker's set of needs and wants. And this group of businesses, while functioning as independent firms, may be involved in other Collaborative Communities that satisfy other sets of needs and wants such as those of joggers, hunters, and athletes. Nonetheless, when focusing on hikers, this group will work together as closely as possible so that the hiking consumer is satisfied and the member businesses in the community operate profitably. The more tightly the community integrates itself, gathering information from the end user, analyzing it, and distributing it among all the member firms in the community, the more satisfied the customers are and the more profitable all the members of the community become.

In essence, the Collaborative Community affords each business member transparent access to information—from product design to product delivery. Significantly, this flow of information throughout the Collaborative Community also allows the end consumer transparent access, from product design to product delivery, and thus gives the consumer the means to provide input to the business members of the community on how best to satisfy his or her personal needs and wants.

In addition, this multiple community participation provides its participants the opportunity to share information across the various communities to which they belong (as long as they don't violate trust and confidentiality agreements). The accrual of this shared information is a valuable asset to every member of the community and, in most instances, will enhance each business's ability to operate successfully in all of its other communities.

As the needs and wants of consumers change, the composition of the Collaborative Community itself must change, and the way each business in the community operates must change. The goal, of course, is to change in a manner that continually leads to an increased ability of the community to profitably satisfy consumers.

THE CHOREOGRAPHER

Each Collaborative Community requires at its core a business that acts as the leader-organizer-coordinator of all the businesses involved in the community. We call this leader-organizer-coordinator the *choreographer*. Given the number of businesses and consumers that may be involved in any one Collaborative Community and that Collaborative Communities can change and transform themselves rapidly, as well as the consumer's lack of time, bewildering choices, and unwillingness to share information with businesses it doesn't trust, the choreographer's most important job is to serve as the interface between businesses and consumers.

The choreographer is therefore the entrepreneur of the Collaborative Community. The choreographer *is the company* that builds the business infrastructure around the set of consumer needs and wants.

> The choreographer builds the business infrastructure around the set of consumer needs and wants.

We call the leader of the Collaborative Community a choreographer because the skills required to accomplish the goals of the Collaborative Community are similar to those required of a choreographer. *Encyclopaedia Britannica* describes choreography as "the art of making dances, the gathering and organization of movement into order and pattern. The choreographic process may be divided for analytical purposes (the divisions are never distinct in practice) into three phases: gathering together the movement material, developing movements into dance phrases, and creating the final structure of the work."[1]

We use the metaphor *choreographer* because just as a choreographer in a musical must select different dancers for different roles, ensure that all of the dancers follow the same rhythm, and encourage every dancer to work together to accomplish the same goal, the choreographer of the Collaborative Community assembles all of the required businesses to satisfy a set of needs and wants, arranges these businesses to function in coordination and synchrony, and motivates each business to accomplish its goals profitably.

Consequently, the choreographer's job is to do the following:

- Recognize the set of needs and wants that defines the community
- Strive to capture 100 percent of the business of *that* specific community of interest
- Facilitate the closed-loop bidirectional flow (represented by the double-headed arrow in Figure 6.1) of information, goods, and services that provides the complete satisfaction of the set of needs and wants of each consumer
- Help all businesses within the community operate profitably
- Understand and follow the iterative process of building a business and community

In Part Three, we discuss each of these components of the choreographer's job, demonstrate the planning tools the choreographer uses to build a Collaborative Community, and examine the information and business infrastructure of the Collaborative Community.

Dell as Choreographer

To provide a better understanding of the general role played by the choreographer and of the choreographer's mindset, let's look at Michael Dell and Dell Computer.

Dell Computer Corporation has introduced a broad range of Dell-branded online services for small and midsize businesses—

everything from direct mail and accounting services to a marketplace where its customers can purchase furniture and cleaning supplies. We see Dell as the choreographer orchestrating a Collaborative Community of a specific group of consumers—small to midsize companies that have a set of needs and wants related to using the Internet in their businesses. As the choreographer, Dell is in the position of bringing into the community other businesses required to satisfy that group of consumers' complete set of needs and wants.

In announcing the services, Michael Dell said, "What distinguishes Dell as a leading provider of technology and services at the core and edge of the Internet is the massive credibility we've built by applying Web-based tools throughout our own business."[2] Combining that knowledge with the understanding that comes from its direct customer relationships gives Dell the expertise and the trust to guide its consumers to the goods and services they need to be successful in the networked economy.

As the choreographer, Dell sees the patterns in the information it collects and then develops an understanding of how those patterns translate into goods and services needs. Using that understanding, Dell goes to such companies as DigitalWorks, AT&T, and OneCore to work out a mutually profitable relationship by which, through Dell, those companies can provide the goods and services Dell itself does not. Because the consumers in the Collaborative Community are the intended customers of the partner companies, this relationship gives every supplier (and Dell as the choreographer) the opportunity to share in, and add to, their knowledge of the consumer. In the networked economy, such knowledge reduces risk and increases profits.

<www.dell.com/us/en/bsd/topics/segtopic_eworks_closed_000_eworks_bsd.htm>

Now that you have a better understanding of the role the choreographer plays in building a Collaborative Community, it is important to stress why we view the choreographer as the entrepreneur of the community. Just as an entrepreneur structures a business, the Collaborative Community is the business model the choreographer structures so that the community can satisfy customers' personal needs and wants. However, as the Dell example shows, you do not have to be an entrepreneur starting a new business to benefit from this new business pattern. Quite the contrary, we believe that *regardless of how long you've been in business, no matter how many customers you have, or what your company's revenues and profits are, you can and should embrace the Collaborative Community as the business pattern for achieving success in the networked economy.* As we have discussed, the Industrial Age business models that have shaped present-day thinking are vestiges of another era and are already dying.

What we need are new business structures and new thinking. Of course, how successful entrepreneurs think—their mindset— has always been the fertile ground for business innovation. So what then is the "right" mindset to achieve and maintain success in this new, customer-controlled economy?

HOW YOU THINK MATTERS MOST

As we mentioned in Chapter 3, the critical mindset for achieving and maintaining success is rooted in what we call the four building blocks of business: process, customers, information, and timing.

Let's look at each one in order.

Process: Is your thinking geared to getting it right the first time or getting it right eventually? We've seen that you will never get your business model right the first time. Never. Thinking you can is simply wrong. Successful businesses are built from instant feedback and adjustment cycles. The message is clear: Don't bet your company's future on a specific business model, no matter how well that model *has* done or *is* currently working.

Success in business comes from engaging in an iterative and intuitive process that allows a business to grow and iterate its business model as customers and the business environment dictate.

What is this intuitive and iterative process? Most simply, it is attempting to develop a business model that satisfies your customers' needs and wants, testing the business model in the marketplace, learning from that test, and then refining the business model to more accurately fulfill your customers' needs and wants. And then you must continue to follow this process of iteration over time (see Figure 6.2 for an overview of the process,

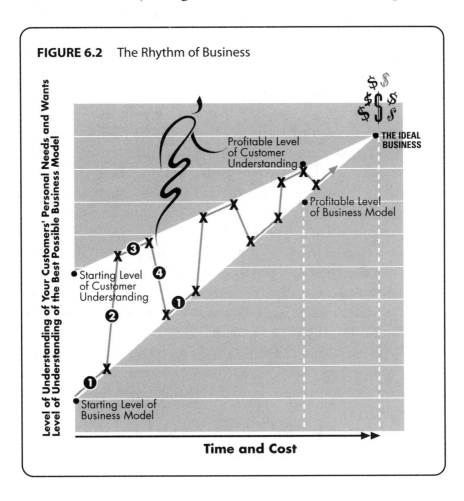

FIGURE 6.2   The Rhythm of Business

and refer to *The Rhythm of Business: The Key to Building and Running Successful Companies* for a comprehensive discussion of the process).

> Most simply, the process is attempting to develop a business model that satisfies your customers' needs and wants, testing the business model in the marketplace, learning from that test, and then refining the business model to more accurately fulfill your customers' needs and wants. This process of iteration never stops.

As you can see in Figure 6.2, the vertical axis reflects your level of understanding of both your customers' personal needs and wants and the business model best able to satisfy those needs and wants. Also shown are the starting points for your level of understanding. The horizontal axis tracks the critical time and money resources. The object of the process is to get to the point shown as "The Ideal Business"—the balance point—where your business profitably satisfies its customers' personal needs and wants better than anyone else in the world. And it needs to do that as quickly and inexpensively as possible.

Because customer needs and wants change as well as do the technological, economic, social, and political environments, success is never final. You can never stop the process no matter how profitable your business is. Once you do, your company will soon be heading down the road to failure.

The iterative nature of the process is represented in Figure 6.2 by repeating cycles that we refer to as "customer interaction cycles." Every customer interaction cycle is composed of four distinct steps.

Step 1: Planning. This step identifies the business model best able to validate your critical assumptions and determines the business and information infrastructure and the resources needed to carry out your plans as quickly and for as little money as possible.

Step 2: Preparation. In this step you do everything that has to be done to prepare to "open for business." This includes identifying potential customers, developing your product, hiring a team, building relationships with the partners you need, putting in place the infrastructure, developing a profit formula, and obtaining financing.

Step 3: Interaction. This step involves bringing your offering to the marketplace and interacting with your customers. Giving your customers an opportunity to actually purchase what you sell is the only way to tell if you are really able to satisfy their needs and wants. So, no matter how long you've been in business, every time you interact with your customers you should consider that you are "testing" your business model's underlying assumptions.

Step 4: Analysis and Refinement. In this step you evaluate the results of the customer interaction carried out in Step 3 and, based on that analysis, refine your understanding of your customers' needs and wants and your business model.

The positioning of Step 1 in Cycle 1 of Figure 6.2 reflects your beginning the business-building process. Step 2 is where you are preparing to interact with your customers. Step 3 is when you actually interact with your customers (i.e., you are open for business), and Step 4 is when you analyze the information gathered in Step 3 and then refine your assumptions about your customers and your business model. As you can see from Figure 6.2, every customer interaction cycle follows a rhythm—as you try out new assumptions, test the assumptions, analyze the results of the tests, and then develop better and better assumptions of your customers' needs and wants and the business model that profitably satisfies those needs and wants.

The steps are shown in a linear fashion to reflect the order in which your thinking should progress at any given time rather than becoming distracted by the many varied activities your company may actually be engaged in. In other words, except when you're in your very first cycle, all of the steps may be in play at once. But your thinking needs to move sequentially as indicated in the diagram. For example, in one product line you may feel you have gathered enough information from paying customers inter-acting with your business (Step 3) to move on to the next step, analysis and refinement (Step 4), even though the company is (you hope) continuing to interact with paying customers (Step 3); and other product lines are in the preparation stage (Step 2); and still other product lines are in the planning stage (Step 1).

The "Xs" on the diagram reflect the transition points in your thinking. It is important to know that when to take the next step is where your intuition comes into play (as discussed later in this chapter). For now, it is only important to understand that there are two aspects to each customer interaction cycle: The knowl-edge aspect consists of knowing that the process is comprised of cycles and that each cycle has four steps; the intuitive part of the process consists of the understanding of *when* to take the steps (i.e., your sense of timing).

In life, there are actions you take according to a preset sched-ule. You get the oil changed in your car every three months or every 3,000 miles. You graduate from school after a certain length of time and after passing a certain set of requirements. But when you build a business, no one tells you when to take a step. Your gut feeling, your intuition about your business, indeed your sense of timing is all that guides you.

Fortunately, no matter how good or bad you think your tim-ing is, following this iterative business-building process improves your sense of timing and enables your company to quickly try, quickly learn, and quickly adapt. Anything else leads to failure.

Meg Whitman, president and CEO of eBay, describes the process used at eBay this way:

> The other critical difference in running an Internet com-pany is our closeness to our customers. This is especially true for eBay, because we enable individuals to do business with one another in a way that's completely new and powerful. As the

medium for that new marketplace, we need to be extremely sensitive to our customers' needs. To do that, we use our instant-customer-feedback mechanism as much as we can: We try out ideas on thousands of customers at once, using live discussions or instant customer surveys. We get products into the community as quickly as possible; then we listen to reactions to those products and make changes accordingly. Some of our best ideas—like feedback profiles, which are now central to our service—have come from our community.[3]

Customers: Is your thinking geared toward beating the competition or satisfying your customers? Underlying the thinking of many corporate executives and entrepreneurs is the belief that their companies need to not only be better than the competition but, to use the jargon of war, to destroy the competition. In fact, many businesspeople frequently use such terms as *destroy, strategy,* and *tactics* that are borrowed from military lingo. It's not that using these war metaphors are wrong. Business does sometimes feel like a battle. The problem is that with repeated use, metaphoric images take on a life of their own and can influence decisions and actions more than we realize.

Unfortunately, war metaphors ignore the most important aspect of business: satisfying the customer. Business is not about beating the competition. In fact, you can beat your competition and still not satisfy your customers, leaving room for another business to steal customers from you and your competition. For instance, if you and a competitor are in the manufacturing business battling each other on price, another manufacturer could win your customers' dollar, if what your customers really want is faster turnaround time or longer warranties.

> Business is not about beating the competition; it's about satisfying the customer.

Of course, we're not saying that you shouldn't identify your competition and analyze what they do well and then try to do better. You need to do that in the process of building and running a business. But if your main focus is on being better than your competition, you are focusing on the wrong thing. *Satisfying your customers is the only way to achieve lasting success and realize the full profit potential of your business.*

So, if you want to build a business that's best able to achieve and maintain success, you had better put away your weapons and lace up your dancing shoes. And remember it's the customer who leads.

As much as businesses give lip service to satisfying customers, it's amazing how many businesspeople actually think in terms of pleasing themselves. To help you understand what we mean, let's take a look at James, a friend of ours. He was getting ready to open his new business—an 11,000 square foot beauty salon and day spa. In his salon, he had set aside an area for 19 manicure and 6 pedicure stations. Obviously, he was thinking big. Setting up the area was really pretty easy. All he had to do was decide where to place the worktables and the chairs for the manicurists and the customers.

James had invited us along to take a look at his place, and we watched with interest as he picked up a manicurist's chair, placed it where he wanted it, then sat in the chair and looked around. After a few seconds, he got up, moved the chair slightly and again sat in it. Satisfied, he then carried over the worktable and the customer's chair. After the first station was in place, he picked up the second manicurist's chair and went through the same routine. After he had done this about five times, we stopped him and asked why he was careful to sit in every manicurist's chair. He said he sat in the manicurists' chairs so he could evaluate whether they would have an enjoyable view. Because the manicurists would be sitting in the chair for eight to ten hours a day, he wanted to make work as pleasant as possible for them.

Was he sitting in the right chair? In addition to sitting in the manicurists' chairs, shouldn't he also have sat in the customers' chairs? James didn't think so. When we asked how he decided which chair to sit in, he reminded us that he had been a hair stylist for years, which gave him an appreciation of what a long workday it was for a manicurist. The customers were going to be in the chair for only a few minutes. Unfortunately, James's business did not succeed.

Information: Is your thinking based on hit-or-miss information or the constant gathering and processing of information?

It's been said that the typical businessperson receives about 150 e-mails, faxes, and voice mail messages per day. The problem with so much attention being put on staying connected is that after a while you tune out when people talk about the importance of information. And that's unfortunate. Because building and running a successful business requires understanding the importance of information and realizing that it isn't so much a word or a revolution. It's a technique.

In its most general sense, information is anything—anything discerned by your senses and intellect. It is every idea, theory, conjecture, experience, or philosophy; and it can be found anywhere—books, magazines, TV, computers, movies, people, and so forth. But the value of information is not in having access to it through the latest technogadget running at the fastest speed. The value of information is when you "gather, process, and connect it."[4]

> The value of information is when you "gather, process, and connect it."

Gathering, processing, and connecting information is taking in random pieces of information and transforming them into knowledge and understanding (refer to Figure 2.2). That's something we all do instinctively every day, but rarely do we examine exactly how it's done. Of course, it's not done in a book or on computer or on the Web. It's done in our heads. We process the information, which means thinking about it, analyzing it, putting it in a comprehensible form. Then we connect it. We see what it's telling us. That means seeing the patterns in the information.

Seeing the patterns in information is a lot like the game of connect the dots we played when we were kids. Think of every dot as a bit of information. When you start, the paper is full of separate dots. As long as the bits of information remain separate, the design on the paper is meaningless. As you connect the dots, as you process the information, the design on the paper becomes clearer until, finally, you have enough lines to see the pattern, to have an understanding, to get an idea. Sometimes you can figure out the pattern with only a few lines. Sometimes you need more lines. Sometimes you need all the lines. But eventually the light dawns. And remember, the person who wins the game is the person who sees the pattern first. And it's just the same in business. The businessperson who wins the game is the one who sees the patterns first and incorporates them into his or her business. It may be creating a new product, or a new Web site, or a new, inexpensive way of manufacturing, or discovering a new customer need. But the point is that most people still pick up information in a haphazard fashion. They might own the latest technology that everyone says they should own, but they do not actively engage themselves in gathering, processing, and connecting information. However, when you're in business you can't rely on accidents or be lazy in your thinking. You have to make gathering, processing, and connecting information part of your life.

We are fortunate that technology allows us to gather more information than ever before, but even with PCs and the Internet, we still have to gather the information, and even then we have to process and connect it; and that takes a lot of time and energy. Nonetheless, it has to be done. It's true that a lot of important information comes by accident because we don't always know the source of the next piece of information or even what it will be. But if we work hard at gathering information and do it all the time, we will find that more and more information comes by accident. And soon we'll realize it's no longer an accident but a technique, a method. It becomes second nature. We'll do it regularly and we'll do it well, but we *always* have to do it.

In Chapter 10 we talk about some of the specific technologies that are revolutionizing the technique of information gathering. These new systems are Web-enabled and browser-based platforms capable of effortlessly automating your company's business processes and intelligently tracking your key data points and metrics, providing the right information to the right people at the right time. Many of these systems can send data to wireless devices, such as cell phones, personal digital assistants (PDAs), and pagers, so that you can "hear" your cash register ring. This new breed of software is easily adapted to match your organization's desired operating environment and provide you with the capability to alter your business processes "on the fly," based on understanding gained through the real-time information generated.

So, talk to friends and cab drivers. Read magazines, surf the Internet, and go to trade shows. Gather, process, and connect information wherever and whatever way you can. Think about the information. Think about your business in new ways, from new angles. What if . . . what if . . . what if. . . . Most people go through this stage when they're writing their business plan. But gathering, processing, and connecting information about your business is not a stage. It's not something you do while you're writing your business plan, trying to impress investors and then forget. You have to do it all the time. There's no getting around it. Information is vital to building a successful business and a Collaborative Community.

Timing: Is your thinking based on structured or intuitive timing? As noted earlier, timing is everything in business. But what hasn't been understood until now is how you develop the ability to move at exactly the right strategic moment—not a moment too soon or too late. In the absence of understanding how to tell when it's time to take a step, many people have resorted to using arbitrary measures of time. For example, they prepare three-year to five-year business plans, 12-month budgets, conduct quarterly reviews, and the like. The difficulty is that timing cannot be preplanned.

The dictionary defines *timing* as "selection or the ability to select for maximum effect of the precise moment for beginning or doing something." And that preciseness of timing cannot be predetermined.

In most business schools and business publications, no one delves very deeply into the subject because, other than preplanning models, no one knows how to explain or teach timing.

We feel we can.

We've discussed how building a business is a process, and as with any process, you need to identify specific predictive metrics that you can track and use to allow you to assess whether your business model is achieving the results you desire. To continue the simple example we used in Chapter 1, you might decide to use the frequency of the cash register ringing as the metric to track how well your customer acquisition process is working. Obviously, if the register doesn't ring frequently enough, you're not attracting customers, and thus some of the assumptions you made about how to attract customers aren't valid and need to be changed.

The key timing question is—How long does it take for you to realize that your assumptions are right or wrong? That is, how many rings do you have to hear before you decide to change your assumptions, or stated the way we prefer, how long do you have to wait between rings before the silence tells you that you have to iterate your business model?

The length of time it takes to decide that an assumption is valid or else is in need of change determines how much information you gather and is therefore a measure of your sense of timing. This sense of timing—knowing the exact moment, the exact point

> The sense of timing—knowing the exact moment, the exact point in which to take action—is based on a combination of intuition and experience.

in which to take action—is based on a combination of intuition and experience, skills you can't learn in school. And that's because you need to feel it—that's right, the way you know when it's time to do something is when you feel it in your gut—literally. How many times have you done something and later been asked why you did it and you responded by saying, "It felt right"? And you meant it. In your gut you had a feeling and you acted on it. And that's because a feeling is your intuitive sense of something, and timing is simply when you put your intuitive sense into action. As we've said, you can't learn these skills in school. You have to develop them from your own experience in business. No matter how good or bad your timing skills currently are, however, you can at the very least make sure you have the right information and most precise metrics available to you in real time, so you can make the best decision possible given your current level of intuition and experience—that is, your current sense of timing. But we have also said you can improve your sense of timing. How do you do that? Well, it's not by reading books or going to business school.

Timing is an abstract quality and can only be developed in an abstract manner. But abstract or not, timing is real and it can be developed as anyone can tell you from their own experience. There's an old saying that's relevant: "You need to love your business." Why? Because the more you love your business, the more you'll stay in constant touch with it and thus the better you'll learn to feel its pulse. The metrics of your business are its pulse. Like a mother feeling the pulse of her child, her sense of whether the child is sick is very accurate based on her love for, and her constant attention to, her child. Her love and attention make up what we can call her child-raising experience; and it is the combination of her love, attention, and experience that develops her intuition. It's the same in business. Your love, attention, and experience develop your gut feeling about your business. If you don't love your business, if you don't pay constant attention to it, if you don't have experience with every aspect of it, your gut feeling is never going to grow.

Again, the above is abstract, but it is real and true. And developing your sense of timing can be written into a real and true formula:

- Love your business.
- Stay in constant contact with it.
- Feel its pulse (i.e., keep track of its predictive metrics).

If the above three points are followed, over time your intuitive sense of timing about your business will grow.

Thus, we've seen that building a successful Collaborative Community in the networked economy requires the skills of a chore-

> Building a successful Collaborative Community in the networked economy requires the skills of a choreographer coupled with the mindset of an entrepreneur.

ographer coupled with the mindset of an entrepreneur. We've also seen that the Collaborative Community is the business structure that today's visionary entrepreneurs are building as the vehicle to satisfy the needs and wants of knowledgeable and empowered customers on a personal basis. In Part Three we'll take a closer look at how a choreographer actually uses the iterative and intuitive process to build a successful Collaborative Community.

To Reiterate . . .

1. Visionary entrepreneurs are developing seamless alliances with the businesses best able to provide the goods and services that satisfy the personal needs and wants of their customers. This networking of consumers and businesses holds the potential to create powerful virtual communities of shared interests and vast economic potential that we call *Collaborative Communities.*

2. Think of the Collaborative Community as the value creation process for the networked economy.

3. In essence, the Collaborative Community affords each business member transparent access to information, from product design to product delivery. Significantly, this flow of information throughout the Collaborative Community also allows the end consumer transparent access, also from product design to product delivery. It thus gives the end consumer the means to provide input to the members of the community on how best to satisfy his or her needs and wants on a personalized basis.

4. As the needs and wants of consumers change, the composition of the Collaborative Community itself must change, and the way each business in the community operates must change.

5. The choreographer is the entrepreneur of the Collaborative Community. The choreographer builds the business infrastructure around the set of consumer needs and wants.

6. Consequently, the choreographer's job is to

   - recognize the set of needs and wants that defines the community;
   - strive to capture 100 percent of the business of *that* specific community of interest;
   - facilitate the closed-loop bidirectional flow of information, goods, and services that provides complete satisfaction of the set of needs and wants of each consumer;
   - help all businesses within the community operate profitably; and
   - understand and follow the iterative process of building a business.

7. Success in business comes from satisfying customers' changing personal needs and wants profitably. And the way to do that is to engage in an iterative and intuitive process fueled by learning from paying customers.

8. Most simply, the process is an attempt to develop a business model that satisfies your customers' needs and wants, testing the business model in the marketplace, learning from that test, and then refining the business model to more accurately fulfill your customers' needs and wants. And then continuing this process of iteration over time.

9. The iterative nature of the process is represented by cycles that we refer to as customer interaction cycles, each of which is comprised of four distinct steps. The four steps of every customer interaction cycle are planning, preparation, interaction, and analysis and refinement.

10. No matter how good or bad you think your timing is, following this iterative business-building process improves your sense of timing and enables your company to

quickly try, quickly learn, and quickly adapt. Anything else leads to failure.

11. If your main focus is on being better than your competition, you are focusing on the wrong thing. Satisfying your customers is the only way to achieve lasting success and realize the full profit potential of your business.

12. The length of time it takes to decide that an assumption is valid or in need of change determines how much information you gather and is therefore a measure of your sense of timing. This sense of timing—knowing the exact moment, the exact point at which to take action—is based on a combination of intuition and experience.

13. No matter how good or bad your timing skills really are, at the very least you must make sure you have the right information and most precise metrics available to you in real time so you can make the best decision possible given your current level of intuition and experience—that is, your current sense of timing.

14. Developing your sense of timing can be written into a true and real formula:

    - Love your business.
    - Stay in constant contact with it.
    - Feel its pulse (i.e., keep track of the predictive metrics).

    If the above three points are followed, over time your intuitive sense of timing about your business will grow.

15. Building a successful business in the networked economy requires the skills of a choreographer coupled with the mindset of an entrepreneur.

ENDNOTES

1. *Encyclopedia Britannica,* Britannica.com; <www.britannica.com/bcom/eb/article/0/0,5716,118760+8+110116,00>.

2. "Michael Dell Says Internet-Driven Growth Puts Technology Industry in Early Days of 'Most Exciting' Period," 27 June 2000; <www.dell.com/us/en/gen/corporate/press/pressoffice_us_2000-06-27-nyc-002>.

3. Reprinted from the June 1999 issue of *Fast Company* magazine. All rights reserved. For more information, visit <www.fastcompany.com>.

4. Jeffrey C. Shuman with David Rottenberg, *The Rhythm of Business: The Key to Building and Running Successful Companies* (Woburn, MA: Butterworth-Heinemann, 1998), 44. *See also,* Michael Shane, *How to Think Like an Entrepreneur* (New York: Bret Publishing Limited Partnership, 1994).

PART THREE

The New Business Pattern

The Collaborative Community is a new business pattern. It's not a business model in the usual sense of how a business organizes itself internally within an industry. A business pattern in our view is a way of organizing businesses in their relationship to customers and to one another. As such, the Collaborative Community makes obsolete our thinking about industries and companies as we know them today. *The Collaborative Community is the new business pattern for value creation in the networked economy.*

The Collaborative Community

7

In our introduction to the Collaborative Community in Chapter 6, we described the community as being composed of three major constituencies—consumers, the choreographer, and member firms. Because knowledge of consumers is scattered around the community, the choreographer's job is to bring that knowledge together. And although any company can be part of the community, only the member firm with the ability to understand and earn the trust of the consumer can effectively assume the role of choreographer. Simply stated, the choreographer is the keeper of the collective knowledge of consumers and helps translate that knowledge into the understanding that each member firm needs to operate profitably as a member of its particular community.

And because the choreographer is the entrepreneurial business that organizes the Collaborative Community, the community itself becomes the choreographer's business model. In other words, the choreographer starts with the business pattern we call the Col-

> Because the choreographer is the entrepreneurial business that organizes the Collaborative Community, the community itself becomes the choreographer's business model.

laborative Community and uses that pattern to organize its specific community. Once the choreographer puts the community together, it becomes the choreographer's business model, because in a very real sense the choreographer must consider the entire community of businesses as part of its "company."

THE CHOREOGRAPHER'S RESPONSIBILITIES

It is important to understand that the choreographer itself is also an individual business entity and as such, in addition to organizing the Collaborative Community, has to build its own business, if it is a start-up, or reconfigure its business, if it is an existing business. In the last chapter, we identified five major responsibilities of the choreographer. Let's take a closer look at each of these responsibilities.

> In addition to organizing the Collaborative Community, the choreographer has to build its own business, if it is a start-up, or reconfigure its business, if it is an existing business.

Recognize the set of needs and wants that defines the community. The salient feature of each community is its specific set of needs and wants. Our discussion in Chapter 5 regarding the set of needs and wants that define a community used an interest in Boston sports teams to demonstrate the challenge the choreographer faces in finding the right level of specificity for the set of needs and wants. In general, the level of specificity of the set of needs and wants is a function of a consumer's ability to recognize the community as relevant and to see the value of sharing personal information and a member firm's ability to contribute to the profitable satisfaction of the consumer's personal needs and wants while operating within the Collaborative Community. The job of the choreographer is to find that right level of specificity in the set of needs and wants so that both consumers and business members want to opt into the community.

Strive to capture 100 percent of the business of *that* specific community of interest. In the Industrial Age, marketing focused on helping companies gain market share. In the age of personalization, however, where market segmentation no longer makes sense and companies are focused on individual customers one at a time, the goal has shifted to capturing a 100 percent share of the customer's wallet. As we mentioned in Chapter 5, it is always more profitable to increase the share of an existing customer's wallet than to sell the same amount to a new customer as a result of the savings on customer acquisition costs.

Facilitate the closed-loop, bidirectional flow of goods, services, and information that provides for the complete satisfaction of the set of needs and wants of each consumer. Because Collaborative Communities are organized around a defining set of consumer needs and wants, part of the choreographer's job is to make sure that the consumer members can satisfy their *total* personal needs and wants relative to the defining set of shared interests. This means that the choreographer has to ensure that each consumer has his or her specific needs for goods and services satisfied. By providing the consumers with all that is desired, the solution offered is a closed loop. Consumers won't have to look elsewhere (i.e., outside the community) for satisfaction of that set of needs and wants. Essentially, this may be thought of as providing consumers with one-stop shopping in that they can obtain from the community all that is needed to satisfy that set of personal needs and wants. But to achieve this goal, the choreographer must make sure that the goods, services, and information flows in both directions (i.e., that the consumer can both receive and send). The two-way flow of information, in particular, ensures the closed-loop quality of the relationship. The more information that flows from the consumers to the choreographer and through the choreographer to the member firms, the more the choreographer and the member firms can satisfy 100 percent of the customers' needs and wants.

Help all businesses within the community operate profitably. One of the major lessons coming out of the first cycle of the networked economy is that companies—yes, even pure-play Internet companies—*must* operate profitably. Obviously, operating profitably isn't a new requirement. It has always been the key metric for any business.

The choreographer provides intellectual leadership and economic leverage to the community as a result of the choreographer's knowledge of the consumers and understanding each member firm's competencies. Essentially, the choreographer tells each member firm that by bringing its skill set into the community, the choreographer will share the specific information the firm needs about each consumer. This information allows you to produce exactly what that consumer wants. The choreographer then works with each member firm to make sure that the firm understands its role and is creating its products and services in ways the firm can deliver profitably. As such, the choreographer assists member firms in making better and better assumptions. It's not that the member firms have to be profitable from day one—in fact, it is very likely that they won't be. But they need to have a pathway to profitability that takes them there in relatively short order. A profit formula has to be built into the business model for each business member participating in the community. Otherwise, it makes no economic sense for them to stay in the community, and they will opt out. And without their skill set, the community may lack the ability to satisfy 100 percent of the needs and wants of the consumers in the community.

Understand and follow the iterative process of building a business and community. The choreographer needs to understand and follow the iterative process of building a successful business as described in Chapter 6. This point is important because the

Collaborative Community is no different from any other business model in that the entrepreneur—in this case, the choreographer—isn't going to get it right the first time. Therefore, to get it right eventually, the choreographer has to understand the iterative and intuitive process that is used, not only to build a successful company, but to build a successful community. And, of course, once it is built, the Collaborative Community has to continually iterate because over time it will need to change. Based on any number of factors, including technology, economics, politics, and so on, consumers will opt into and opt out of the community, depending on their changing needs and wants. At the same time, member firms will opt into and out of the community, depending on their ability to continue to profitably provide the solution consumers require.

Now that we've taken a look at the principal requirements of the choreographer's job, it's time get into the specifics of how the choreographer actually goes about the process of building a Collaborative Community. To gain that understanding we start in Chapter 8 by identifying the customer opportunity and then move in Chapter 9 to how the choreographer puts its business model together. In Chapter 10 we explore the underlying business and information infrastructure, and then in Chapter 11 we discuss the resources required to build the choreographer's business and the community.

But before we do that . . .

LET'S MEET CIRCLE COMPANY ASSOCIATES, INC.

One of the points we have stressed is that the Collaborative Community is a *new* business pattern that visionary entrepreneurs are just starting to build. Consequently, we feel that the best way to help you gain a better understanding of how the concepts we're discussing are being operationalized is through a detailed description of one of these new businesses: Circle Company Associates, Inc. (Circles). All of the information about Circles comes from several conversations with CEO and cofounder Janet Kraus and our analysis of several of the company's business plans. Janet and cofounder Katherine Sherbrooke opened for business in 1997, and since 1998, in conjunction with the third principal member of management, Jennifer Guckel, today provide "Web-based personal assistance to companies that are seeking to capture and enhance the loyalty of their customers and employees."

Janet and Kathy got to know each other while earning their MBAs from Stanford Graduate School of Business, where they worked together on several high-profile projects, including their class gift project: conceiving, fundraising, building, and opening the doors of a $94,000 media center in less than four months. Both have significant business experience in marketing, product development, and operations. The company is based in Boston and in mid-January 2001 had 240 employees; 80 customers who make Circles' services available to 1.2 million members; 1 distribution channel partner with 1.5 million members; and 8 top-tier consulting and referral partners. The company has over 30,000 service providers and resources in its database as well as preferred service contracts in place with 75 vendor partners. Circles expects to begin to turn a profit mid-year 2001.

One last point about Circles. None of the authors of this book has had any input in the start, development, and running of its business. Yet, as you will see, in the process of growing in today's business environment, Circles is evolving into a Collaborative Community.

To Reiterate . . .

1. The Collaborative Community, as we see it, is a new business pattern. A business pattern is a way of organizing businesses in their relationship to one another. As such, the Collaborative Community makes obsolete our thinking about industries and companies as we know them today.

2. Although any company can be part of the community, only a member firm with the ability to understand and earn the trust of consumers can effectively assume the role of choreographer. Simply stated, the choreographer's company is the keeper of the collective knowledge of consumers and helps translate that knowledge into the understanding that each member firm in the community needs to know so they can determine how to profitably operate as a member of that particular community.

3. Because the choreographer is the entrepreneurial company that organizes the Collaborative Community, the community itself becomes the choreographer's business model.

Building a Collaborative Community

8

With our current understanding of what a Collaborative Community looks like, including the general role played by its three main constituencies (consumers, a choreographer, and member firms), we turn next to the specific activities a choreographer needs to carry out in building a Collaborative Community as described in Chapter 7. The story of the development of Circles will help us illustrate these activities and also show the iterative and intuitive business- and community-building process in action. Janet Kraus says that in Circles' short history, the company has iterated pieces of its business model 14 times.

To help you visualize what all choreographers need to do, Figure 8.1 provides a framework for the choreographer's business model. We'll use this framework to guide us through Circles' story, describing the major iterations the company has made over time as it gained a better understanding of its customers, their needs and wants, and how best to profitably satisfy them.

Although this framework may at first appear complicated, it really is just another way of looking at how we define success in business. As you may recall, success in business is pretty simple. For customers, success means that their personal needs and wants are satisfied. For companies, success is the cash register ringing (profitably) when a customer is satisfied.

So, let's get started . . .

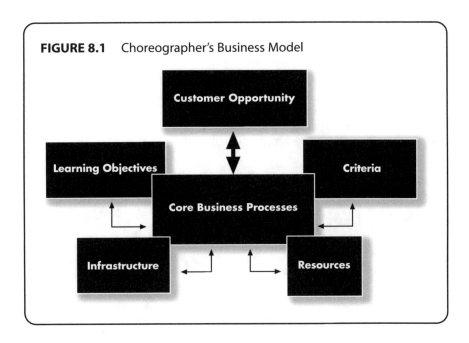

FIGURE 8.1   Choreographer's Business Model

DEFINE THE CUSTOMER OPPORTUNITY

Not surprisingly, given the consumercentric nature of the Collaborative Community, the first activity the choreographer has to undertake is to define the customer opportunity.

The customer opportunity has two elements: the set of needs and wants that defines the community and the goods, services, and information that will satisfy each consumer within the community (see Figure 8.2). In this chapter we look at how a choreographer—and Circles in particular—defines a customer opportunity. The first step is to identify the shared interests of the community.

Identify the set of needs and wants that defines the community. As we saw in Chapter 5, the defining set of needs and wants serves as the basis around which a choreographer builds the Collaborative Community. However, as we said, within any particular set of needs and wants, the choreographer has to determine the "ideal level of specificity" on what we call the needs and wants

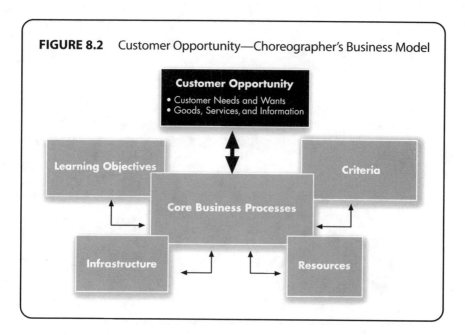

FIGURE 8.2   Customer Opportunity—Choreographer's Business Model

continuum. Finding the balance between making the set of needs and wants narrow enough so that consumers will see the benefit of opting into the community yet broad enough that member firms can make a profit is a primary responsibility of the choreographer. For explanatory purposes, recall Chapter 5, Figure 5.2, Needs and Wants Continuum. In this figure, we designated three levels of detail—broad, narrower, and narrowest—although in reality we are dealing with a level of specificity that may fall anywhere along the continuum.

Even though technology is making it increasingly possible to provide every consumer with exactly what he or she needs, the issue is whether the business structure that provides that solution can do so profitably. The truth of the matter is that identifying the point where any given consumer sees the value of participating in the community, and where member firms and the choreographer can operate profitably, is very difficult to establish. Except in rare instances, that point is only arrived at through practicing the iterative process that leads to greater understanding and thus better assumptions that validate unknowns. The challenge for the choreographer is to understand the iterative process and facilitate it, so that the level of balance is arrived at as quickly and inexpensively as possible and can be maintained as the consumers' needs and the business environment change.

CIRCLES' SET OF NEEDS AND WANTS

But now, let's take a look at how Circles initially focused in on the set of needs and wants it believed it could profitably satisfy.

Circles started as a concept in July 1996. Like many people who were watching the events of the first cycle of the networked economy, Janet Kraus and Kathy Sherbrooke were eager to jump aboard the Internet train, so they started searching for an opportunity. And as smart entrepreneurs, they instinctively knew that the best way to identify a business opportunity was to start with the customer: in this case, themselves. Even though they started with themselves, however, we'll see as we get into the story that they utilized themselves more as models for customer profiles than as representatives of a set of needs and wants. In other words, they focused on themselves as women with a certain level of education, earning capacity, skills, and the like, rather than as individuals with a specific set of needs and wants. This legacy-style assumption led to at least two iterations of their business model before they discovered a viable set of needs and wants. However, using themselves to define a customer profile did get them started and allowed them to arrive at a mission for their proposed Internet company. They expressed that mission as Enhancing the Life of the Professional Woman. With this goal, Janet and Kathy set out to make Circles Online the "ultimate online integrated resource of products, services, and information targeted to simplify and enhance the life of the busy, time-sensitive professional woman."

Here's how they described that woman's needs:

The professional woman is a busy, time-sensitive person who leads a rich and multifaceted life. She highly values her career and measures professional success by her level of effectiveness, her impact, her relationships with employees, colleagues, and customers. Of equal importance to her is having a fulfilling personal life—strengthening her relationships with friends and family (husbands, partners, children, parents), maintaining her health and well-being, making a contribution to her community, and enriching her creative and/ or athletic and/or spiritual life. She defines her overall success and happiness by her ability to be effective in *all* the circles of her life. In her efforts to successfully manage so many competing priorities, this woman seeks resources that understand her needs and offer her solutions in ways that are convenient, save her time, and add value to her life.

Some of this woman's needs are purely professional, others are purely personal, still others are a combination of both. Some examples of the needs that this professional woman has are communicating effectively with business colleagues and customers, balancing her role as a primary caregiver with her strong career, finding ways to make business travel less stressful, running a household while working full-time, ensuring her personal safety when work takes her to unknown places, and organizing and furnishing her office. Each of these needs requires a different level of information, products, and services to create a complete solution.

As Janet and Kathy developed their ideas, they continued to make the underlying assumptions about how to satisfy those needs that would form the first iteration of their business. They spoke with more and more potential customers and collected as much information as they could. Using the technique of gathering and processing information we spoke of in Chapter 6, they saw that the one basic characteristic each woman shared was the lack of time. This new information resulted in a second iteration.

In interview after interview, the busy professional woman will state that in order to help her reclaim some time for herself, what she needs more than anything else is a personal assistant, an alter ego, a clone; in fact, the phrase she used most often to describe the solution to her problems was, "What I really need is a wife."

Professional women tell us that the responsibilities they would most like to make easier or eliminate altogether include grocery shopping, gift buying, dependent care, health and personal care, social event and meal planning, housework, home improvement, car care, clothing care, bill paying, and financial planning.

Noticeably absent from this new description of needs and wants but present in the earlier definition is anything to do with a woman's professional life. The first definition was much broader in its set of needs and wants, for it included effectiveness in business relationships and organizing and furnishing an office. The second definition is much narrower. Virtually all of the items in the second description can be seen as helping to "balance her role as primary care-giver with her strong career, finding ways to make business travel less stressful, running a household while working full-time." Consequently, even before they opened their doors for business, Circles evolved a more specific definition of the set of needs and wants it believed the company could profitably satisfy.

This second definition was the set of needs and wants that Circles began to fulfill when it opened for business in June 1997, almost a year after first seeing a business opportunity. However, assumptions about customers—what they need and want, who they are, where they are, and how to reach them—are just that until customers reach into their wallet. Once open for business and after having served several hundred customers, Janet and Kathy quickly realized they didn't have the financial resources to reach enough time-starved professional women to build a profitable business. In fact, to try to give themselves enough time to develop new assumptions, they drastically cut costs. Janet says, "We sent back the water cooler, and we cut our salaries, and we talked about moving back to my house." Some entrepreneurs would have seen failure plastered all over those actions. Janet and Kathy iterated.

Here is how they next defined the set of needs and wants:

People are busier than ever. Personal tasks that need to be done during the day either don't get done, causing employee lives to become unbalanced, or they are done on employer time, causing a huge loss in business productivity.

High-value employees, who are increasingly in demand, are finding it harder than ever to balance the demands of their personal and professional lives.

Companies understand that their success depends in large part on these employees, and thus recognize that benefits that address personal and professional balance are essential to their strategies for attracting, motivating, increasing the productivity of, and retaining the best. Employees know the tasks they need to get done, but have no obvious way to do so.

Circles has an enormous opportunity to become the supplier of services that answer these needs by contracting with employers to serve as a trusted intermediary between vendors and employees. Circles adds value to all parties by linking its qualified branded vendors to consumers who are willing and eager to buy these products and services and who feel appreciative of employers who make this program available.

Precisely. The set of needs and wants of the consumer community—who the two women now defined as time-starved, high-value employees—is still the same, except that the economic reality of reaching customers one at a time forced a shift in distribution strategy that, in fact, opened up new revenue opportunities. Instead of looking for customers one at a time, Circles saw that they could reach more consumers who had a need for personal services by working through corporations who would then make Circles' services available to their employees as an employee benefit.

This shift in approach is very important because it marks the point where Janet and Kathy changed from focusing on a demographic customer profile, that is, the professional woman, to focusing on a set of needs and wants—getting personal tasks done. This change in focus significantly increased their pool of potential consumers and, although they didn't think of it as such, also marks the point where Janet and Kathy began to take greater advantage of structuring their business as a Collaborative Community. (Although we focus on Janet and Kathy, as we discuss in Chapter 11, building Circles is a team effort.)

Certainly before this point, in trying to satisfy the needs and wants of professional women, Janet and Kathy were making alliances with other businesses. But when they changed their distribution strategy and offered their services to corporations, they gave themselves the opportunity to generate additional revenue streams—a key advantage for a business that assumes the role of choreographer for a Collaborative Community. Now their customers are not only consumers and the service vendors that purchased Circles' enhanced listings but also the employers that are negatively impacted by their employees' unmet personal needs.

In this way we see the company continuing to build its business, learning how to function as a choreographer for its Collaborative Community of consumers (employees whom Circles refers to as members) and member firms (corporate customers and service providers).

As we move through the framework in Figure 8.1, we can see this development more clearly. However, before we do that, we need to consider one more subtle but powerful iteration in the set of needs and wants Circles realized had to be made.

After changing its distribution method to using corporations as the means of providing its services to consumers, Circles ascertained that employers that offered their employees work/life benefits such as Circles' services garnered greater loyalty from their employees. In other words, employers gained a greater share of their employees' professional careers. Lower employee turnover represents a cost saving that falls right to a company's bottom line. Most companies want to reduce employee turnover and increase productivity, but when you distill that need to its essence, companies need to build the loyalty of its employees before they can expect to reduce turnover.

So the set of needs and wants Circles sought to satisfy became broader. It now was not only attempting to meet the personal needs of the employee-consumer community, but it was attempting to meet the needs of employers by generating greater workforce loyalty. In addition, it saw an opportunity to meet the needs of service providers that were struggling to reach consumers: "Essentially, we will be providing a valuable, otherwise unavailable service, to the service provider at a very competitive price. By creating an efficient marketplace for our service providers, by helping them proactively reach our customers, we will essentially create added revenues for them."

Here is another way to look at the sets of needs and wants of the three constituencies that form the Circles Collaborative Community:

Constituency	Definition of Needs and Wants
Consumers	Assistance in completing personal tasks
Corporations	Assistance in building the loyalty of employees and customers
Service providers	Assistance in acquiring customers

THE 100 PERCENT SOLUTION

Now that we have established the set of personal needs and wants that Circles is working to satisfy, it is time to look at the other piece of the customer opportunity as represented in Figure 8.2.

Identify the goods, services, and information required to satisfy the personal needs and wants of the consumer community. As we said, for a community to be successful, ideally consumers must have the ability to fulfill their complete set of needs and wants for goods and services relative to the particular set of needs and wants on which the community is based. While striving toward the 100 percent solution is the goal, the community still has to function successfully at levels less than the ideal. But even though the community may never reach the 100 percent solution, the choreographer must nonetheless try to identify the specific goods and services that constitute a total solution. As we discussed earlier, the shift in the way in which consumers interface with businesses means that consumers expect to collaborate in product development. So the only way the choreographer can hope to identify the 100 percent solution of what should go into the market basket of goods and services is through its collaborative relationship with consumers. Consequently, the choreographer must have the strongest relationship with the consumers in the community. That is, the choreographer needs to establish a loyal, leverageable consumer base built on trust and a capacity to understand the consumer. Once established, that base empowers the choreographer to represent the voice and spirit of the consumer to the team of member firms it brings into the community.

> The choreographer has the strongest relationship with the consumer and establishes a loyal, leverageable consumer base built on trust and a capacity to understand and represent the voice of the consumer to the member firms.

As with everything else that is driven by consumers' needs and wants, the choreographer has to appreciate that from the consumers' perspective, the market basket of goods and services is very dynamic and must be updated as consumers' needs and wants change over time.

CIRCLES' MARKET BASKET

Let's return to Circles and see how Janet and Kathy went about identifying the goods and services they would offer and see how that offering has developed as their understanding of the community's needs and wants has deepened.

As you will recall, when Circles began to create its business model, its initial broad definition of a set of needs and wants was based on those of a professional woman, time starved in both her personal and professional life. Circles intended to provide solutions that would "simplify, add convenience, or enhance feminine style." For a brief period, the company planned to inventory and resell tangible products as well as provide access to services and information. In setting the criteria for product selection, Circles made the assumption that goods would need to be "of high quality, appropriately styled, hard to find, or difficult to purchase currently, and in many cases of unique design." Figure 8.3 reproduces a

FIGURE 8.3   Circles—Product Assumptions, September 1996

Target Areas	Products	Services
Wo-Managing Your Career	• Customized customer gifts • Customized employee gifts • Management books and videos • Motivational products	• Online chats with top executives in your field and local break-out sessions • Sign-up service for local seminars • Recommended training workshops • Professional organization resources
Ensuring Your Personal Safety	• Handheld personal safety devices (panic buttons, whistles, pepper spray, etc.) • Car safety kits • Mobile window alarms	• Sign-up for self defense classes • Online forums on avoiding sexual harassment in the workplace
Time Savers	• Presorted occasion cards • Quickie gifts that say thank you or job well done	• Personal reminder service • Gift-finding service • Monthly stocking delivery
Staying Fit and Healthy	• Relaxation products • Exercise accessories (bags, lunch totes, hair-drying towel, stocking saver) • Nutritional books and videos	• Spa and health club finder • Online nutritional consultations • Online fitness evaluation
Traveling with Ease	• Best luggage for women • Most helpful travel accessories • Car travel accessories	• Links to weather reports and mapping sites • AAA sign-up • Links to travel agencies
Creating a Workspace in Your Style	• Desk accessories • Ergonomic chairs • Prints	• Silk flowers • Bimonthly fresh flower delivery

table from Circles' September 1996 business plan that lists the proposed products and services aligned with each major category of customer need. While this is not the market basket the two women opened for business with, it is nonetheless instructive to understand Janet and Kathy's initial assumptions.

One element of the two entrepreneurs' initial market basket, not abandoned but not depicted in the figure, is the information component, a critical element in providing a complete solution. "One of the characteristics of women as purchasers is that they appreciate having information available to them when they are making purchasing decisions. Circles Online, in its role as value adding aggregator, will enhance our entire offering providing not only sales copy on specific products, but also expert opinions on product categories, third-party recommendations on specific products, and general industry information."

As they were making decisions about the products and services they wanted to sell, Janet and Kathy recognized that they needed to build a learning relationship or, as we would express it, a collaborative relationship with their customers. Here are some of their earliest thoughts on how to go about building that relationship:

> Many of the services [offered] provide an added benefit both to our customer and to us—the building of an intelligent and interesting community for professional women. Community-building activities are an important part of what makes customers build an affinity with the companies from which they buy, and it is often the relationship that keeps them coming back.
>
> Membership is an interesting phenomenon on the Web. At present, people seem very willing to "join" free groups online if there is some apparent benefit. For this they are readily willing to provide significant amounts of data about themselves. This not only gives us valuable marketing data but also offers our customers a chance to find value in being more closely associated with us.

At Circles Online, we hope to take advantage of this phenomenon, asking our visitors to "register" with us for free. For registering their important statistics and preferences, we will provide services such as an occasion reminder service, additional access on our site, and targeted interaction with the customer. We will use this registration process as the first step in developing a relationship with our customer.

As we've mentioned, consumers are now less willing to offer personal information. Later on, when we discuss some of the core processes of the Circles' business model, we will look more closely at how the company collects and protects personal information. So far, however, it has been successful at gathering the personal information it needs. (We should note—as discussed in Chapter 4—customers do not generally object to information being collected if it is used to the customer's advantage; but that information must not be sold to the highest bidder or in other ways distributed without the customer's permission.)

As we saw in the discussion of focusing in on the set of customer needs and wants, Janet and Kathy increased their level of understanding of what potential customers truly desired even before they opened for business. They increased their level of understanding by holding many informal conversations with potential customers, asking open-ended questions in focus groups, and wading through stacks of market research, trade magazines, scholarly reports, and news reports. They also commissioned a statistical market survey. Ultimately, they decided what would best meet the needs and wants of their intended customers was not a handful of nice-to-have specialty products but a "regional database of value-added service listings of service providers that at present are not aggregated"—a sort of Zagat's guide for the personal service industry. It would be a must-have resource, ending the worry of how to get such projects accomplished by speeding up the research and decision-making process relating to service providers. Customers would access the database either over the Web, on Circles Online, or via 800-CIRCLES, a fax-on-demand service. Based on what they had learned from their research (remember in the company's history we are starting from the beginning again and Circles had not yet interacted with paying customers), the company launched itself with a database of several hundred service providers. The following lists a few of the services included:

Dependent Care

Childcare
Elder care
Pet care

House Maintenance and Repair

House cleaning
Interior design/Decorating
Lawn care/Landscaping
Plumbing and electrical
Appliance repair
Carpentry/Construction

Clothing Necessities

Dry cleaners/Laundry
Tailor/Seamstress
Shoe repair
Clothing storage

Shopping Services

Personal clothes shopping
Personal gift shopping
Grocery shopping

Personal and Body Care

Nail salons
Facial and skin care
Massage
Health club/Personal trainer
Yoga/Meditation
Chiropractor

Car Care

Servicing
Mechanics
Car dealers

In making the shift from a product-based offering to a knowledge-based offering, the company eliminated inventory risk. When enough of its customers expressed interest in a specific service, the company could more easily add a category of information in its database than source, purchase, and inventory new products.

Also, in building a superior resource of service providers, the company realized it could build greater knowledge about its customers:

From the day that Circle Company Associates launches Circles Online, the company intends to gain sustainable advantage by collecting, analyzing, and acting on subtle information collected about our customers.

> Through our registration process and our database-searching questionnaires, we will learn where she lives, what she does professionally, what she enjoys personally, whether she works in a corporation or from home, and whether she is married, has children, or travels frequently. . . . We intend to launch our site with an interactive approach that gives our customer the opportunity to help us further define our offering.

This last sentence shows that Circles understands when it comes to determining the personalized goods, services, and information that consumers want, consumers must collaborate in the decision making.

As noted before, within a few months after their launch, economic realities forced Janet and Kathy to rethink how to reach customers. Fortunately, as their consumer-focused business model was put into operation, it began to attract corporate attention. At this juncture, they realized they could better reach customers by having corporations offer Circles' services as a benefit to their employees. However, after making this shift, that iteration of Circles' business required changing its offerings. The following provides some detail of this change:

> Through the application of designated vendor partners, centralized messaging and automation technology, and streamlined marketing and customer service, Circles provides companies and their employees with a reliable, high-quality, personalized, and convenient delivery process that enables employees to accomplish life's pressing personal tasks.
>
> The LifeSavers™ program includes:
>
> - *EasyAuto*
> - *Clothing CareFree*
> - *Personal Express*
> - *Dinners Ready*

- *Grocerytime by HomeRuns*
- *InBalance Message*

The products that Circles brings to companies help alleviate the stress and aggravation in employees' lives by addressing some of the pressing needs on their To Do Lists. From dry cleaning and laundry, to car repair and inspection stickers, to personal errands and assistance services, to fresh meal delivery and onsite chair massage, to a personal help desk for everything from service referrals to tracking down tickets and hard-to-find items, the Circles LifeSavers™ program meets the needs of nearly everyone in a company.

The company also developed a series of specialized corporate offerings to assist with event planning, employee recognition, executive support, and relocation, to name just a few. The following are a few examples of these services:

The Main Event. Many companies consider group activities, whether fun activities and/or community service projects, to be an important part of building and encouraging a committed corporate culture. Circles is expert at planning events of all types—from trips to the ball park, theatre events, dinner affairs, and community service projects.

Right at Home. Circles provides companies with custom-designed "Right at Home Packages," complete with maps, brochures, Circles information on the best service vendors in the neighborhood, and certificates toward service help—like $100 worth of handyman, personal organizing, unpacking, or "wait at home for the cable guy" services.

By the summer of 1999, Circles was responding to 2,000 requests per month, a 720 percent annualized growth rate over the prior six months and LifeSavers™ had become LifeConcierge.com: "A carefully designed and robust portal for activities in a person's life, LifeConcierge.com combines self-serve personal services, features, and functionality *combined with* high-value virtual personal assistance."

The types of services offered was a function of the requests made by its members and the company's ability to find qualified service providers. While these rapidly increased, the number of corporations offering Circles' services (which now included a prominent credit card issuer) also grew.

Today, the depth of the knowledge base Circles has attained from fulfilling the personal requests of 1.2 million members is staggering. "A comprehensive offering of content and services is available through the seamless integration of Circles' proprietary knowledge base, Personal Assistants, and preferred partner sites." In October 2000, the company offered to its members the services shown in Figure 8.4.

FIGURE 8.4   Circles—Product Assumptions, October 2000

SAMPLING OF SERVICES

ENTERTAINMENT	**HOME**	**SHOPPING**
Activities and events	Contractors and handymen	Art
Adult education	Decorators	Baby/Children
Community involvement	Electricians and plumbers	Books, music, and movies
Event planning	Grocery and meal delivery	Clothing
Health clubs	Housecleaners	Cookware
Restaurants	Internet and wireless service	Drugstore
Spas and salons	Landscapers	Electronics
Tickets	Laundry delivery	Fitness and sporting goods
AUTO	Movers and storage	Flowers
Buy and sell	Painters	Gift ideas
Car rental	Pet care	Health and beauty
Cleaning/Detailing	Realtors	Home goods
Insurance plans	Utility comparison	Jewelry
Repair and maintenance	**TRAVEL**	Lawn and garden
ERRANDS	Airfare	Luggage
Dry cleaning and shoe repair	Car rental	Pet supplies
Drugstore	Limo and car service	Stationery/Greeting cards
Pick up and drop off	Passports and visas	Toys
Post office	Places to stay	Wine
Wait at home	Sightseeing tours	Product comparison
	Vacation planning	Hard-to-find items
	Weekend getaways	

As a choreographer, Circles satisfies the needs and wants of its service providers, corporate customers, and consumers.

To its consumers, Circles offers time-saving personalized goods and services. To its corporate customers, Circles offers the value proposition of greater loyalty from employees. For service providers, Circles offers knowledge and understanding about prospective customers, helping service providers hone their product offerings to match the individual needs of consumers as well as furnishing the service providers with easy and inexpensive access to a pool of consumers they might otherwise never have reached.

> To its consumers, Circles offers time-saving personalized goods and services. To its corporate customers, Circles offers the value proposition of greater loyalty from employees. For service providers, Circles offers knowledge and understanding about prospective customers and easy and inexpensive access to a pool of consumers.

Not surprisingly, technology plays an ever increasing role in Circles' success. As product development becomes virtually synonymous with technological development, the company is maximizing the value it offers to its three revenue-generating constituencies—corporate customers, service providers, and members—by leveraging the value of knowledge of the community for all members of the community. We speak more about this later, but for now let's continue our walk through the choreographer's business model.

To Reiterate . . .

1. The defining set of needs and wants serves as the basis around which a choreographer builds the Collaborative Community.

2. The customer opportunity contains two elements: the set of needs and wants that defines the community and the goods, services, and information that will satisfy each consumer within the community.

3. Identifying the point where any given consumer sees the value of participating in the community, while at the same time member firms and the choreographer profit, is very difficult to establish. Except in rare instances, that point is only arrived at through practicing an iterative process that leads to greater understanding and thus better assumptions about how to validate unknowns.

4. The only way the choreographer can hope to identify the 100 percent solution of what needs to go into the market basket of goods and services is through its relationship with consumers. Consequently, the choreographer must have the strongest relationship with the consumers in the community.

5. The choreographer needs to establish a loyal, leverageable consumer base built on trust and a capacity to understand the consumer. Once established, that base empowers the choreographer to represent the voice and spirit of the consumer to the team of member firms it brings into the community.

The Choreographer's Business Model

9

In the previous chapter we identified a customer opportunity as the set of needs and wants that defines the consumer community and (in collaboration with consumers) the goods, services, and information that satisfy consumers on a personal basis. The choreographer's job is to use that understanding to build a community that can operate profitably.

We now turn our attention to Figure 9.1, the Core Business Processes of the Choreographer's Business Model. In designing a business model, we think of the business as being composed of three interrelated core business processes:

1. Customer acquisition and retention process—how a community gets and keeps customers
2. Product and service innovation process—how a community continuously generates the goods, services, and information that will satisfy customers
3. Customer fulfillment and service process—how a community delivers to and supports customers

It is our belief that everything a business does is either part of these core processes or part of the business and information infrastructure discussed in the next chapter.

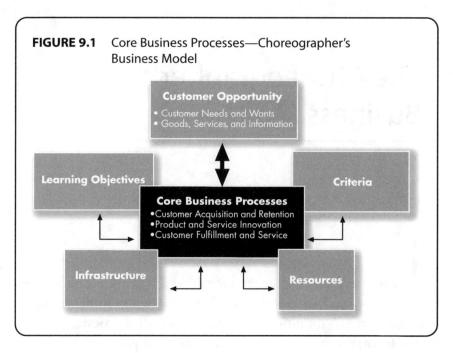

FIGURE 9.1   Core Business Processes—Choreographer's Business Model

It is absolutely critical that all three core processes be designed from the consumer's perspective. That means that they must all start with the customer and then work their way through the value creation network. Much has been written about business process design and businesspeople are familiar with such terms as "business reengineering" and "lean thinking." These approaches had their place in 20th century business models in which the company dominated, but with a knowledgeable and powerful consumer in the 21st century, the legacy approach of designing processes that start in the company and end with the consumer won't work.

DESIGNING THE BUSINESS MODEL

Because we are at the point of designing the business model, we are still focused on Step 1 (planning) of The Rhythm of Business (Figure 6.2). In this step, assumptions come into play once again as a business model (the three core processes) is nothing more than a hypothesis through which you test your assumptions.

The choreographer develops the initial version of these processes by making a number of assumptions based on its level of understanding of the customer opportunity. The choreographer must make sure that when it begins to interact with customers the processes will generate the information needed to assess the validity of the assumptions on which the processes are based. Therefore, as seen in Figure 9.2, the choreographer should

- identify *all* of the assumptions on which each process is based;
- rank order the assumptions by their relative importance as some assumptions are more critical than others; and then

FIGURE 9.2   Assumptions Grid

Core Business Processes

Validate
Y or N   **Customer Acquisition and Retention Assumptions**

1. _____
2. _____
3. _____
4. _____
5. _____
n _____

Product and Service Innovation Assumptions

1. _____
2. _____
3. _____
4. _____
5. _____
n _____

Customer Fulfillment and Service Assumptions

1. _____
2. _____
3. _____
4. _____
5. _____
n _____

List by order of importance

- select the specific assumptions that it's hoped will be validated in the current customer interaction cycle.

Every time the choreographer redefines the customer opportunity, it needs to go through this sequence of action for each core business process.

The choreographer then moves into Step 2 (preparation), putting into place the thousands of details required to operationalize the business through the core processes. Then, in Step 3 (interaction), when actually operationalizing the core processes, the choreographer uses its information infrastructure to track key metrics to allow it to assess how well the individual processes are working. In Step 4, the choreographer learns by performing the necessary analysis and refinement of what occurred in Step 3—that is, in Step 4, the choreographer evaluates the assumptions made in Step 1 by comparing them to the actual metrics generated in Step 3, which either validate or invalidate those assumptions. If the assumptions on which any process is based are proven to be invalid, the choreographer uses its new level of understanding to make new assumptions. Then, employing those new assumptions, the choreographer modifies the process in light of the newer and better assumptions. (Back to Step 1 again.) And over time the whole process is continually repeated, each cycle shaping the business model to permit greater satisfaction of customers' personal needs and wants and higher profits.

Now let's take a closer look at each of the three core business processes in a general sense before returning to our discussion of Circles in greater detail.

Customer acquisition and retention process: How the choreographer plans to get and keep the community's customers.
Once a customer opportunity has been identified, the choreographer must develop its assumptions about how to bring consumers into the community and keep them there. One of the benefits of the Collaborative Community is that, while the choreographer is responsible for developing a trusted relationship with consumers,

the community's business members assist in bringing consumers into the community.

Let's look at what a customer acquisition and retention process should include from a general standpoint. The choreographer should do the following:

- Collaborate with prospective customers to identify how the community will satisfy their personal needs and wants relative to the community's shared interests
- Create awareness through publicity and marketing
- Identify leverageable relationships to reach customers
- Generate prospective customers
- Begin the process of building trust with each customer
- Assist member firms in communicating with customers
- Facilitate collaboration in the development of a personal solution to every consumer's needs and wants
- Actually get customers to engage in a transaction within the community
- Collect feedback from customers about their degree of satisfaction and communicate the results as required to the business members in order to better satisfy customers, thus retaining them within the community

It is important to again stress that in the age of personalization, it makes much more sense for the choreographer to use the set of needs and wants as the driver in acquiring customers rather than going after a specific customer profile. Ultimately, the goods and services that the community provides must satisfy customers on an individual basis. Thus, the choreographer should start with the set of needs and wants and then use this set of shared interests to assist in the identification of individuals who have that set of needs and wants. Then use the acquisition and retention process to bring those individual consumers into the community.

Product and service innovation process: How the choreographer plans to develop the stream of goods, services, and

information offerings to satisfy customers' changing personal needs and wants. Essential to the smooth functioning of the community is the choreographer's ability to orchestrate the continuous innovation of goods, services, and information desired by consumers. The choreographer accomplishes that task by collaborating with member firms and with consumers to develop personal solutions. As we saw in Chapter 7, a key aspect of the choreographer's job is to facilitate the closed-loop bidirectional flow of information, goods, and services within the community. Member firms use the choreographer's access to customers and information about the customers to help them profitably provide personalized solutions.

What are the components of a product and service innovation process? The choreographer must do the following:

- Collaborate with customers in identifying their specific needs and wants
- Encourage members of the community to develop ideas regarding new ways to satisfy customer needs and wants
- Allow for the development and testing of ideas for new products and services in collaboration with customers and member firms
- Facilitate the commercialization of products and services that meet customer needs and wants
- Monitor customers' experiences with the products and services and communicate that experience to the appropriate members of the community (and their network of suppliers) in order to adjust and refine the product and service offering
- Develop and introduce new products and services that will satisfy customers' changing needs and wants profitably

At the end of the day, this process determines whether the choreographer will successfully identify and put in place a profit formula. Without the *continuous* satisfaction of consumers, the choreographer and member firms will not sustain a profit and the community will not survive. Consequently, the rubber meets the road in the community's innovation process.

Customer fulfillment and service process: How the choreographer plans to distribute to and support the community's customers. In the networked economy, the watchwords for fulfillment and service are *anytime anywhere*. The ability of the choreographer to accomplish the *anytime anywhere* requirement is based on the bidirectional flow of goods, services, and information among all members (businesses and consumers) in the community. The choreographer uses the community's business and information infrastructure to facilitate that flow.

From a general standpoint, to structure the customer fulfillment and service process, the choreographer should do the following:

- Collaborate with customers to identify the ways in which they wish to access the community's product offerings
- Facilitate the bidirectional flow of goods, services, and information
- Provide the service and support necessary for customers to achieve an enthusiastic experience with the community's product offerings
- Monitor customers' experiences with fulfillment and service, and communicate the resulting information to the appropriate members of the community in order to adjust and refine the fulfillment and service operations

Now that we have an overview of the core business processes, let's see how they work in a practical way as demonstrated by the methods Circles is using to build its Collaborative Community.

CIRCLES' CORE PROCESSES

As we've seen, Circles has three "customers": members (consumers)—individuals who benefit from Circles' services; corpo-

rate customers (member firms)—companies that purchase Circles'
services to build the loyalty of their customers and/or employees;
and product and service providers (also member firms)—the
businesses that perform the services and provide the products for
Circles' consumer customers and pay Circles for access to consumers. Depending on the agreement the company has with any
one corporate customer, the members (consumers) may pay for
certain services. Figure 9.3 represents Circles' business model of

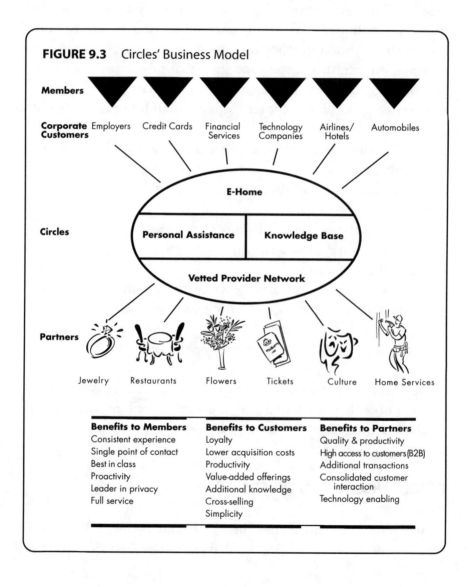

FIGURE 9.3   Circles' Business Model

October 2000 and the power of the Collaborative Community—a value proposition for all participants in the community. Because each of the core business processes begins with the consumer and works its way through the value creation network, these different members of the Collaborative Community play an important role in all of the core business processes.

The Collaborative Community aids Circles in acquiring and retaining customers in the following ways:

- Corporate customers bring consumers into the community by offering Circles' services to its employees and customers.
- Consumers bring service providers into the community when they request new services.
- Service providers keep consumers in the community by fulfilling their needs.
- Consumers keep corporate customers in the community by remaining loyal to the corporate customer.
- Consumers keep service providers in the community by continuing to request services.

This set of interconnected relationships shows how the Collaborative Community can benefit everyone in the community. In a practical sense, it also shows that the focus of Circles' customer acquisition efforts must be on bringing corporate customers into the community. To accomplish this end, the company uses both a direct sales force and channel partners. The direct sales force and channel partners approach companies that it is hoped see the value in Circles' services for their own customer/employee acquisition and retention. In addition to sales efforts, the company's marketing strategy is designed to generate awareness and credibility with potential corporate customers. The company has had several high profile media placements, including *Fast Company, Fortune,* and *Forbes,* exhibits at a number of trade shows, and was selected to present at Springboard 2000, a highly selective venture capital forum.

The company has a responsibility to its service providers, not only to bring consumers into the community by signing up corporate customers, but also to have consumers use the services. Although the percentage varies from company to company, approximately 50 to 70 percent of the consumers who can avail themselves of Circles' services in any given company do so, a percentage far greater than their competitors achieve. From the perspective of the corporate customer, the greater the percentage of employees/customers who participate, the more successful the program. Consequently, one of the challenges the company faces is to understand the range of services it can offer in response to employees'/customers' requests versus their ability to profitability offer that desired range of services. Really, the question is one of finding the profitable level on the needs and wants continuum as we saw in Chapter 5.

The company continues to test in order to find that balance while marketing directly to its members to build program awareness, generate new memberships, and increase the use of its services. This marketing program highlights another benefit of the Collaborative Community. While at the corporate offices during one of our interviews with Janet Kraus, we observed the company in the process of putting together a beautifully designed direct mail piece to go to nearly 25,000 employees at selected corporate customers. But this was one direct mail piece the Post Office would never see. To get the piece to its customers, Circles was utilizing its member companies to place the brochure on each employee's desk. Talk about personal. And that partnership saved the company about $10,000 in postage and mailing costs.

The company has put significant resources into researching, developing, and adding to its base of service providers. Thus, only a small portion of the 30,000 service providers have actually been brought into the community as a result of a unique request from a member. In addition, Circles does not currently generate revenue from every service provider. As Janet put it, currently the administrative cost of collecting a fee from the "dog walker in Tuscaloosa" is greater than the fee it would receive for the referral. However, the company does have formal relationships with the 75 service partners who handle the lion's share of requests and they do pay for access to, and knowledge about, consumers. (We'll talk more about this in the next chapter in our discussion of the relationships between the choreographer and the member firms.)

Customer retention is critical for every business but even more so to Circles' business because, as we've seen, it is a key part of their value proposition to corporate customers. Keeping the consumers (the employee members), of course, begins the moment the corporate customer joins Circles' community and that retention process starts with building trust. As we saw in Chapter 4, trust is necessary in order for customers to share the information required to satisfy personal needs and wants. Circles begins to build trust with its employee members by asking them to provide only the information necessary to fill a specific request. "We want it to be as painless as possible to just get in and get started," says Janet.

Over time, Circles increases its knowledge of its members and is thus able to provide them with the exact service provider to satisfy their personal needs. For example, if Circles knows, on the basis of a prior request, that a member has exotic water plants in his or her Japanese garden, it offers the member a service provider who understands the care and feeding of exotic water plants the next time the member requests a landscaping contractor. Soon the company intends to provide smart messages for members, such as birthday and anniversary reminders—perhaps even messages that it's time to winterize those exotic water plants. This knowledge will be developed both through information that members provide directly and information gleaned from knowledge of member requests and the solutions provided to them.

Circles also builds the trust of its members through the quality of its service provider referrals. In essence, the referral communicates to the service provider only the personal information the provider needs to deliver excellent service. The company is fanatical about service excellence. Here are some of the requirements that must be met to become a Circles' service provider:

- Punctuality and reliability
- Follow-through on all promised tasks

- Complete and forthright delivery of the appropriate level of information at all times
- Delivery of high-quality work
- Listening to the needs of the customer
- Being upfront about any limitations or issues as they develop
- Exceeding expectations at every possible opportunity
- Respecting each and every customer, including the customer's time, property, and privacy
- Determination to make each interaction with a customer a positive one
- Being resourceful about meeting the needs of the customer

Consumer members are asked to complete an evaluation of every request. Despite its rapid growth, Circles' members are satisfied with the service they have received 99 percent of the time. That builds trust and keeps customers coming back!

Next, let's turn to Circles' product and service innovation process. Janet nicely sums up the objective of innovation within the company:

Just imagine in life that any particular company was relevant to you and actually knew about you and was able to proactively help you think about things that you needed, or that some company became a resource for you about lots of things in your life. That's what we want to be for our end users. And we want to be able to help our partners *know* about our end users in a way that respects their privacy.

Not surprisingly, from the customer's perspective, a big piece of Circles' innovation process takes place within the customer acquisition and retention process. Every new request made by a member is an opportunity for product and service innovation. You will recall that part of the job of the choreographer is to facilitate the bidirectional flow of products that personally satisfy consumers and also to help every member of the community operate profitably. So part of Circles' innovation relates to the value the company offers to consumers and part relates to its relationships with member firms.

We noted in our discussion of the customer acquisition and retention process that constant personal communication with members supplies a wealth of information about the services they need and want. This regular contact not only also provides greater customer satisfaction but helps identify the services consumers request most and enjoy the most. Knowing these top services then allows Circles, in conjunction with its corporate customers, to create the best programs for their employees. In fact, part of the sales process is to work with its many corporate customers to develop programs personalized specifically for each company. In addition, the personal communication with service providers has allowed the company to forge close relationships with certain "preferred" providers.

Of course, while Circles devotes a great deal of its resources to developing the products and services that satisfy the personal needs and wants of its members, both the company and its service providers know the key is to do it profitably. Accordingly, much of the innovation process involves the use of technology to:

- Maximize revenue opportunities by creating an offering that is attractive to all constituents—corporate customers, consumer members, and service provider partners
- Improve operating margins through automation, process controls, etc.
- Increase barriers to entry through continued development of core proprietary assets (e.g., knowledge base, virtual personal assistants, recurring contracts)
- Increase consumer member usage through additional portal features, functionality, personalization, and promotions

As Circles notes:

Future technology releases will maximize efficiency and scalability by increasingly automating the service delivery so that workflow in the Solution Center is as automated as possible, and end users have the option to use self-serve solutions directly from the site. By building, licensing, and integrating the technologies that increase the automation of transactions handled by live PAs [personal assistants], we are focusing on achieving the biggest productivity improvements in the shortest time frame possible. The ultimate vision is to deliver a very high-value, customized solution that is 75 percent automated.

A third element in the company's innovation process relates to the use of its rich databases. As we've said, Circles has information about the personal needs and wants, and solutions to those needs and wants, of 1.2 million members and a database of more than 30,000 service providers and partners.

Part of the value the choreographer offers is the depth of consumer understanding required by member firms so that they (and the choreographer) can operate profitably. While Circles has yet to share any analysis of consumer behavior, this knowledge and understanding can help reduce risk for member firms by providing them with the ability to forecast demand and plan better purchasing as well as develop more personalized and relevant direct marketing. Circles is just beginning to explore other opportunities to utilize these databases to further product and service innovation for their partners and members—a key benefit of a Collaborative Community.

The last of the interrelated core business processes we need to look at is the customer fulfillment and service process. Again technology plays a big part in delivering the solution to customers and, as time goes on and Circles becomes platform independent (accessible over the telephone, the PC, or wireless devices), technology will play an even greater role.

In fact, Circles' fulfillment process offers us a great example of how advances in communication and information technologies that have raised customer expectations have also enabled businesses to respond to these increased expectations. Circles itself does not "do" any of the services it offers to its members. It fulfills a member's request by finding the best-qualified partner or service provider—generally one already included in its database—to fulfill the actual request. What Circles does do is use technology to separate the information or knowledge part of its service from the product or service part. By partnering with service providers to actually deliver the solution to members' personal needs, Circles focuses on its competence—locating or creating the solution—and the service providers focus on their core competencies—landscaping, housecleaning, event planning, and so on. This focus on "doing what you do best" is an essential component of the Collaborative Community because it helps all of the business members in the community to be more profitable.

When you think about it, Circles' role as a personal assistant means that customer service *is* the business. Why else would it have a VP of Service Excellence?

Circles sees its focus on service as a critical differentiator in the market—both from competitors and substitute services.

Circles Personal Assistants are educated, bright, articulate, and responsive with terrific judgement and impeccable customer care skills, who customers trust, enjoy working with, and want on "their team." The core capability of all Service Delivery team members is to help customers create simple, time-saving solutions out of time-consuming situations. Each member of the Service Delivery team will go through four weeks of specific job training, followed by on-going refresher courses, and frequent peer and Team Leader feedback sessions to keep skills exceptionally high.

Through careful process design, and detailed protocol development, Circles has created a delivery mechanism and system to consistently provide high quality personal assistance.

With a phone call or an e-mail, a Circles member can get virtually anything accomplished. The company's e-mailed quality control questionnaire at the conclusion of every service supports partners and service providers in their efforts to offer stellar service. Service and support is a process of learning to do better from the customer's perspective. As a choreographer, Circles helps each service provider do better with each customer contact. And that helps Circles.

The quality control questionnaire is a key data-gathering tool in the company's efforts to become successful. It provides Circles, from a member's perspective, with the information it needs to analyze and refine (Step 4) as needed, after *each* customer interaction (Step 3). Here is a sample from Circles' questionnaire:

Please rate the degree to which your expectations were met in each of the following (labeled a-e), using the following scale:

4 = Exceeded expectations
3 = Met expectations
2 = Did not quite meet expectations
1 = Failed to meet expectations
   a. Ease of placing your request
   b. Quality of services performed
   c. Timeliness of service
   d. Value for fees charged
   e. Attitude of concierge

If your expectations were not met, would you like a member of the Circles' management team to contact you?

Using the following scale, please rate the extent to which using the concierge service . . .

4 = Significantly
3 = Moderately
2 = No/NA
1 = Negatively
   a. Reduced your stress level
   b. Helped you stay focused on work
   c. Made you feel that your company is a good place to work

How many hours do you estimate you saved using Circles?

Certainly not all members return the questionnaire. Those that are returned provide valuable data about how to better evoke the enthusiasm of all members.

IDENTIFYING THE BEST CORE PROCESSES

Because there are undoubtedly many different ways to configure each of the core processes, the choreographer has to carefully think through each possible configuration and then decide which is best for that process. The question is, What criteria should be used to make that decision? In the end, there is no real way to assess the effectiveness of the processes except by actually using them and comparing the assumptions on which they're based against real-world results. Testing assumptions by interacting with paying customers is one of the fundamental tenants of the iterative process of building a successful business. However, the choreographer should nevertheless, as part of its decision-making process, evaluate each of the process options against the criteria shown in Figure 9.4.

> Testing assumptions by interacting with paying customers is one of the fundamental tenants of the iterative process of building a successful business.

PROCESS CRITERIA

The key criteria that the choreographer should use to identify the best option are iterability, people, scalability, time, and cost.

Iterability: How easy is it to iterate? Given that the core processes are iterated cycle by cycle, it is important to make sure they are designed with as much "iterability" as possible. In this context,

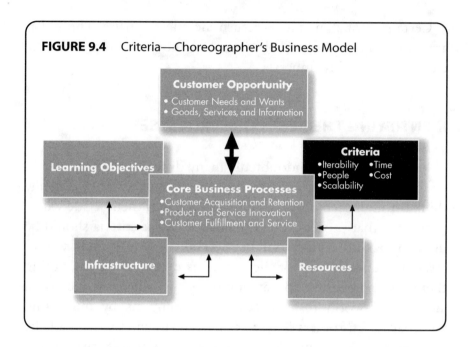

FIGURE 9.4   Criteria—Choreographer's Business Model

it is generally better to keep costs variable rather than fixed, to buy versus make—in other words, to put as few "stakes in the ground" as possible. The structure of the Collaborative Community supports this criterion because, as we've seen, Circles doesn't actually perform the personal services. Thus, it doesn't have to invest in the infrastructure to support a corps of service providers. In fact, we've seen that Circles has turned the cost of a service provider infrastructure into a revenue stream. Of course, not all choreographers or Collaborative Communities will have the exact same business structure as Circles, but the point is that the Collaborative Community is a community, and the less each company has to commit in terms of fixed resources, the more flexible the entire community is. And as the community itself is based on a confluence of synergies between each member firm, the synergies will naturally result in cost savings and less need for capital investment.

People: How available are the people skills needed?   People are a scarce and critical resource, so it is essential to identify the specific skill sets needed to effectively operationalize each core process and then to assess the likelihood of bringing to the team the people with those skills. It is of no value to try to implement a process if the choreographer cannot get access to the people skills needed. For example, one of the challenges Circles faces is the ability to hire enough personal assistants with impeccable customer care skills. Otherwise, the company will not adequately build the trust of its members and the community will not succeed.

Scalability: Will the process scale as the business grows? Because the choreographer is attempting to take full advantage of the customer opportunity by growing the community, it is important to make sure that the process will work under an increasing level of activity. In other words, is it scalable or will growth be constrained at some point? Accordingly, it is better to use processes that can scale in usage as the volume of activity increases. As we've seen, Circles' customer acquisition process is scalable because it leverages its relationships with corporate customers to increase its member base. And its innovation and fulfillment processes are becoming more scalable as it makes greater and greater investments in technology.

Time: How quickly will things happen? Although we now know that Internet time isn't as fast as some people thought it was, remember that the choreographer is trying to get smart (i.e., make better assumptions) quickly, for time is a precious resource. Consequently, all things being equal, the faster a process validates or invalidates assumptions, the better.

Cost: How much does the process cost? The choreographer has to evaluate the cost-benefit tradeoff of each of the processes. Knowing the cost of a process and the availability of the money to cover that cost is critical. Remember, the horizontal axis on Figure 6.2 reflects time and cost. As such, the choreographer is trying to get smart as quickly and inexpensively as possible.

Obviously, these last two criteria are resources a business can never afford to run out of. For example, Janet and Kathy almost lost their business when in their first year they found that trying to acquire individual consumers one at a time was too costly and time-consuming. Thus, they were forced to look for—and, as we've seen, found—a customer acquisition process that was more "resource friendly." If they had known their business was going to iterate 14 times when they wrote their first business plan, they might have planned—that is, reserved resources—for further change. As it is, they were fortunate and serendipitously found their more resource-friendly method of distribution/customer acquisition. Understanding the iterative process of building a business is vital to planning time and cost criteria because you will then know that time and cost do not just include the present iteration of your business model, but that to some degree you must plan for the time and cost involved in future iterations. (We'll talk more about this in Chapter 11.)

LEARNING OBJECTIVES

Clearly, while the five criteria are all very important, the choreographer must also evaluate each of the core processes in terms of whether its use will lead to achieving established learning objectives. Learning objectives should enable the choreographer to get smart quickly for short dollars. Thus, an additional two factors relate to whether each core process will allow the choreographer to assess if the business is hitting the key milestones necessary to realize profitable growth and whether sufficient information is being generated to validate the critical assumptions on which the process is based (see Figure 9.5).

Let's discuss each of these factors in turn:

Assessing whether the core processes will enable the business to hit key milestones necessary to realize profitable growth. Seven categories of milestones are important to the choreographer:

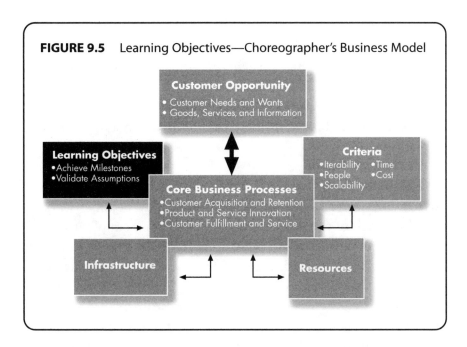

FIGURE 9.5   Learning Objectives—Choreographer's Business Model

1. *Customers:* Is the community acquiring and retaining sufficient customers?
2. *Key management and team:* Have key management and team members been recruited?
3. *Strategic partnerships and alliances:* Have the necessary strategic partnerships and alliances with member firms been put in place?

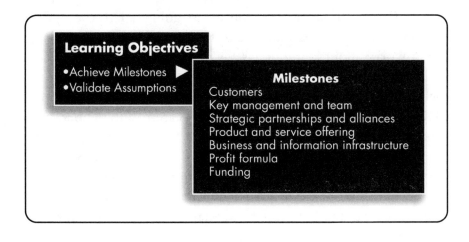

4. *Product and service offering:* Are the goods, service, and information desired by the customers being developed?
5. *Business and information infrastructure:* Is the required business and information infrastructure in place?
6. *Profit potential:* Has a profit formula been identified?
7. *Funding:* Has the needed funding been obtained from the right investors?

Validating the critical assumptions on which the process is based. Of course, as we said, there are many possible ways to configure each of the three core processes. For example, the choreographer could design the customer acquisition and retention process by employing a direct sales force as the primary means to sign up new customers. Alternatively, the choreographer could use its partners (i.e., member firms) to bring customers into the community as we saw in the case of Circles. Or the choreographer could use a direct mail campaign to attract new customers. Or a television and radio campaign. Or it could use a combination of methods. Although these options represent only part of the overall customer acquisition and retention process, they nevertheless demonstrate that the choreographer has many choices from which to design the specific process to be used in each interaction cycle.

So how can the choreographer decide beforehand which option to use? As a tool to assist in evaluating each option identified for each of the core processes, the choreographer uses Figure 9.6 to compare and rank each option by assigning a 1 to the option that is believed to be best and a 2 to the second best, and so forth. Don't worry about being precise as this is a subjective evaluation procedure. And while the decision of which option to use for each process should not be based solely on the ranking totals, this tool forces the choreographer to be very careful and deliberate in making the decision.

Furthermore, while the five criteria identified are all very important, we believe that the two learning objectives are, in the scheme of things, of much more significance. If the choreographer is not hitting the milestones and validating the core assumptions,

FIGURE 9.6   Process-Ranking Matrix

Customer Acquisition and Retention Process
Options

Criteria	1	2	3
Iterability	___	___	___
People	___	___	___
Scalability	___	___	___
Time	___	___	___
Cost	___	___	___
Learning Objectives			
Achieve Milestones	___	___	___
Validate Assumptions	___	___	___
Total	___	___	___

Product and Service Innovation Process
Options

Criteria	1	2	3
Iterability	___	___	___
People	___	___	___
Scalability	___	___	___
Time	___	___	___
Cost	___	___	___
Learning Objectives			
Achieve Milestones	___	___	___
Validate Assumptions	___	___	___
Total	___	___	___

Customer Fulfillment and Service Process
Options

Criteria	1	2	3
Iterability	___	___	___
People	___	___	___
Scalability	___	___	___
Time	___	___	___
Cost	___	___	___
Learning Objectives			
Achieve Milestones	___	___	___
Validate Assumptions	___	___	___
Total	___	___	___

time and money are being wasted, because unless the assumptions are tested, there is no basis for knowing how and when to iterate the core processes.

> If the choreographer is not hitting the milestones and validating the core assumptions, time and money are being wasted.

Remember that the three core business processes are developed expressly to find the balance point between the level of specificity in the set of consumer needs and wants that defines the community and the ability of the choreographer and member firms to operate profitably. Consequently, each time a change is made to that balance point, the core processes (i.e., the choreographer's business model) may have to be iterated. In addition, when any one of the core business processes is iterated, it will likely have an impact on the other core processes, so each of the other core processes must again be evaluated to see if they, too, need to be iterated.

Once the core processes have been designed, the choreographer must next focus attention on the business and information *infrastructure* and the *resources* needed to build the community profitably. In Chapter 10, we discuss the business and information infrastructure, and we explore the resources required in Chapter 11.

To Reiterate . . .

1. When we look at designing a business model, we think about the business as being made up of three interrelated core business processes:

   1. Customer acquisition and retention process—how a community gets and keeps customers
   2. Product and service innovation process—how a community generates the goods, services, and information that will satisfy customers
   3. Customer fulfillment and services process—how a community delivers to and services customers

2. It is absolutely critical that all three core processes be designed from the consumer's perspective. That means they must all start with the customer, work their way through the value creation network, and then work back to the consumer.

3. Without the *continuous* satisfaction of consumers, the choreographer and member firms will not sustain a profit and the community will not survive. Consequently, "the rubber meets the road" in the community's innovation process.

4. There is no real way to assess the effectiveness of the processes except by actually using the processes and comparing the assumptions on which they're based against real-world results. Testing assumptions by interacting with paying customers is one of the fundamental tenants of the iterative process of building a business.

5. The key criteria that the choreographer should use to identify the best process option are iterability, people, scalability, time, and cost.

6. The choreographer must make sure that engaging in a process will generate the information needed to assess the validity of the assumptions on which that process is based.

7. If the choreographer is not hitting the milestones and validating the core assumptions, time and money are being wasted because, unless the assumptions are tested, there is no basis on which to know how and when to iterate the core processes. Remember that the three core business processes are developed specifically to find the balance point between the level of specificity in the set of consumer needs and wants that defines the community and the ability of member firms to operate profitably.

Business and Information Infrastructure

10

To guide our thinking, in this chapter we once again use the choreographer's business model. However, our attention needs to drop down a level as we get into the particulars of identifying the detailed components of the business and information infrastructure (Figure 10.1). In Chapter 11, we consider their resource implications.

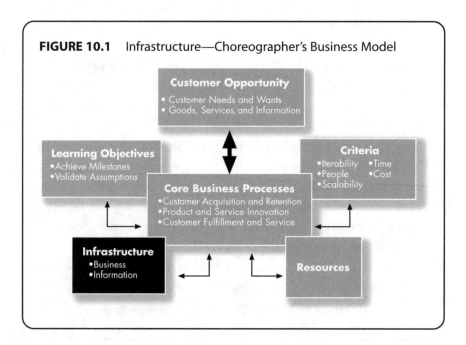

FIGURE 10.1 Infrastructure—Choreographer's Business Model

Every time the choreographer iterates the three core business processes in trying to find the right level of balance between satisfying the consumers' set of needs and wants and profitability, the underlying business and information infrastructure that supports those processes may also need to iterate. This is because every set of core business processes is supported by a *unique* business and information infrastructure.

BUSINESS INFRASTRUCTURE

Now that the choreographer has identified the three core business processes, it is time to plan (Step 1—planning) and then actually build (Step 2—preparation) the business infrastructure needed to make the community work. The diagram below identifies the five major components of the business infrastructure that we explore:

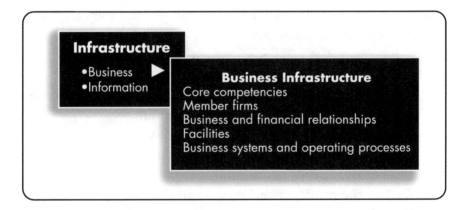

Core competencies: Identify the core competencies needed within member firms and the choreographer's business for the community to function successfully. After the choreographer has identified the specific goods, services, and information to be made available to consumers, it must next identify the competencies specifically required to produce/provide what is desired. Essentially, the choreographer is starting with the desired output of goods, services, and information and then working through the value creation network for each item so that the specific competencies needed to provide personal solutions can be determined. This is not the same as trying to identify particular companies that could provide the products desired, for competencies are people-embodied skills. To actually deliver any given product solution may require the competencies aggregated from a number of companies as well as from independent businesspeople, a category of individuals that has come to be known as *free agents*.

In addition, the choreographer has to identify the competencies needed to operationalize the business and information infrastructure for its community. As with the competencies needed to produce a personal solution for each consumer, the choreographer must identify the specific skills needed within both the member firms and itself to execute the core business processes, to put in place the supporting business systems and operating processes, and to make appropriate use of the enabling technologies.

The competencies required within any Collaborative Community are unique to that community, but in general they are those that will accomplish the following:

- Develop the trust of the consumer
- Understand the consumer's personal needs and wants relative to the shared interests of the community
- Bring the consumer into the community
- Develop the products and services that satisfy the consumer's personal needs and wants
- Deliver the products and services to the consumer
- Provide the support and service customers require
- Keep the consumers and member firms in the community
- Develop the business and information infrastructure required to support the community
- Develop the relationships required to operate the community
- Obtain access to the resources required to operate the community
- Operate the community profitably
- Iterate as customers and the business environment change

Every choreographer must develop this list specifically for the customer opportunity it is attempting to satisfy. Then the choreographer must determine the skills required to accomplish these objectives. Some competencies it will develop or already possess; for the others, it will identify a potential member firm to partner with to bring that skill into the community. While the choreographer is responsible for ensuring that all of these competencies are present within the community, they can be aggregated among member firms and shared with the choreographer. However, if we think back to our description of the choreographer's job in

> The choreographer is responsible for ensuring that all of the required core competencies are present within the community.

Chapter 7, there are certain skills the choreographer's business must possess. These are the competencies required to accomplish the following objectives, which are a subset of the preceding list:

- Develop the trust of the consumer
- Understand the consumer's personal needs and wants relative to the shared interests that define the community
- Develop the business and information infrastructure required to support the community
- Develop the relationships required to operate the community
- Obtain access to the resources required to operate the community
- Operate the community profitably
- Iterate as customers and the business environment change

Along with the ability to recognize the patterns in information, the most important skill a choreographer can possess is the ability to negotiate. Whether it's raising money from investors, working with customers, or bringing member firms into the community, almost every aspect of putting together a successful Collaborative Community involves negotiation. Accordingly, the choreographer needs to understand the importance of negotiation skills and practice developing them.

Circles' Competencies

Identifying what any company does best requires experience and learning as the business grows and develops, so it is likely that the sharing of competencies between the choreographer and the member firms will change as the core business processes iterate. Over time, Circles has learned that it is best at creating personal solutions for customers. "One of our core competencies [is] our ability to understand and to respond to the customer's unique set of needs," says Janet Kraus. The company excels at finding the best-in-class providers of those services and connects them with members at exactly the time the member needs the service. This is how Janet describes a few of the competencies Circles and its partners possess:

Program development, and behind that is organizational flexibility to be what the consumer needs you to be. Ours is a competency of having the right resources. A financial services company is not going to have a relationship with a ticket company. That's way too far away. And my program for a [financial services company] might look measurably different than my program for an [airline]. It is just a process of [personalizing] the components to get the program correct because it is going to look different customer by customer. And as a result of that, as you're working with a customer, you realize that you need to add to this; you'll go out and find them then. So it is a network. It is a collaboration of different players.

You may not recognize [our partners], and the reason you don't recognize these brands is that these companies focus on product and delivery, and they don't focus much on marketing. They've decided as a business model that they're going to focus on product and delivery. They're not in the business of trying to build brand. And so I'm promising you quality.

Circles orchestrates the network of more than 30,000 service providers to produce personal solutions for its members. Through the use of technology, the company tracks the competencies of its providers and matches them to the personal needs of its members. We'll take a look later at the information infrastructure that makes this work, but Janet is clear that technical excellence is something they are continuing to strive for: "We don't yet have in place the technology to do all the things that we want to do." It all takes time and money.

In addition to the competencies required to directly fill members' requests, Circles, like any company, needs to bring together the competencies to operate the community. This includes not just technology providers but also skills in design, advertising, finance and accounting, legal issues, and more. In other words, between its employees and a group of member firms we'll call *enablers,* the skills to develop and profitably utilize the business systems and operating processes must be included in the community.

Earlier we spoke of the trust that consumers need to develop in a choreographer before sharing their personal information. However, the choreographer also needs to develop trust in the member firms' ability to provide the personal solution the consumer requires. While every Collaborative Community will be different, this is critical in the case of Circles because of the direct contact its member firms have with the consumer. If the house painter provided through Circles does a terrible job, it is Circles that has failed a customer. In order to put a service provider into a member's home, Circles has to trust the service provider.

Circles needs to ensure that its partners deliver the level of customer service its members expect. Accordingly, it developed service provider guidelines, which we reviewed in Chapter 9, to describe the competencies in service delivery the company expects from its service providers.

Member firms: Identify the specific business entities. After the choreographer has identified the competencies needed by the community, it must next identify the specific business entities that possess those competencies and recruit them to be member firms, whether they are free agents or Fortune 500 companies.

Interestingly, Circles has found other choreographers who are aggregating smaller service providers, creating their own Collaborative Communities. Circles is integrating many of these smaller Collaborative Communities into its larger Collaborative Community and is considering how to make its combined alliances even more seamless. Janet explains:

> When we first started, we had to be the niche aggregator. We had the dog walkers and the plumbers. What has happened, luckily for us, is that now there have been companies that have gotten into that business for a particular niche and so they have all the good folks. We could do warm handoffs to them—be our local services specialist. And it would be blind to our customer.
>
> The roll-up of other industries is really important because they've focused on the real depth of the taxonomy. In the beginning we had to focus on a narrow set of issues because we couldn't go that deep, whereas now we have the ability to partner with people who go that deep.

It is that depth of competency that is needed to profitably provide a personal solution to consumers.

Essentially, the message a choreographer brings to a potential member firm is that in return for bringing its skill set into the community, the choreographer provides access to consumers and shares specific information about them and other member firms, thus allowing the potential member to produce exactly what consumers need; in addition, the choreographer helps the firm operate profitably.

Of course, not all member firms join the community for access to consumers. Some member firms may actually themselves provide access to consumers. In the case of Circles, these firms are its corporate customers. Here's what Circles looks for in this type of member of its community:

- Firms that employ highly skilled, highly sought-after employees with a pressing need for timely access to quality personal services
- Firms that rely on intellectual capital and billable hours as their means of production
- Firms that pride themselves on their treatment of employees
- Companies that seek to provide personal services as a commodity differentiator, purchase stimulator, data-mining tool, or marketing program
- Companies that, by the nature of their product, interact infrequently with their customers and want to build stronger relationships with them
- Companies that see value in extending their relevance by adding personal services to their offering

The other type of member firm that must be identified are the enablers, the partners that help power the community. In the beginning, Circles partnered with Web development and design firms to build its Web site. Today it is partnering with firms that allow members wireless access to Circles' e-service portal, that automate Circles' sales force, and that help Circles obtain media placements intended to create awareness of the company.

As the needs and wants of consumers change, the composition of the Collaborative Community itself may change and the way each business in the community operates may change. The goal, of course, is to be able to iterate in a manner that continually leads to an increased ability of the community to profitably satisfy consumers.

Business and financial relationships: Structure the choreographer's relationship with member firms. Having identified the desired member firms, the choreographer next has to structure its business and financial relationship with each entity. As we discussed in Chapter 7, the choreographer must facilitate the closed-loop, bidirectional flow of goods, services, and information that provides for the complete satisfaction of the set of needs and wants of each consumer as well as ensure that each member firm can operate profitably. How the choreographer structures the business and financial relationships will impact the ability of the community to be successful.

As part of this activity, the choreographer must focus on the thinking of each member firm. That is, just as the choreographer has to think like an entrepreneur, the member firms need to think of themselves as part of a community of competencies that selectively come together to satisfy an individual consumer's personal needs and wants.

This community of aligned businesses requires each member firm to

- view its business from the perspective of the customer;
- cooperate with other member firms and the choreographer;
- allow the maximum flow of, and be willing to share, information; and
- iterate its business model as customers, technologies, and economic conditions require.

Most important, the choreographer has to make sure there is an alignment of interests (e.g., a desire for profit) among all member firms in the community so that they work as a team, a team that's focused on the personal satisfaction of the consumers.

In addition, the choreographer has to provide intellectual leadership to all member firms in the community. Because of the choreographer's access to information from the consumers as well as from all the member companies, the choreographer has the most information. That depth of information empowers the choreographer to use its knowledge and understanding of all member firms to make the best use of that information to fulfill the personal needs and wants of consumers on a profitable basis for all the business entities in the community.

The choreographer faces many technical and operating challenges relating to the sharing of information among the member firms. We will look at some of the technical challenges in a moment, but for now let's examine the operating challenges. Member firms will belong to other communities, so what is to say that they won't use information learned in one community to help succeed in another? To some degree they will. Intel sells computer chips to both Dell and Compaq, and you can be sure it uses understanding developed with Dell when working with Compaq and vice versa. What must be protected by strong upfront agreements is proprietary information. Like any relationship, the bond with member firms will grow over time, and more will be shared. Just as the choreographer provides information to a member firm, the member firm will provide information about its customers, capabilities, and challenges to the choreographer. And just as in a customer relationship where loyalty is built by relevance and performance, the longer the Collaborative Community operates together profitably, the greater the loyalty will be among its members. Plus, the more a member firm is integrated into the community in terms of its business and information infrastructure, the less likely it will move to a competitive community.

In addition, as the community strives for 100 percent of the consumers' dollars, it becomes more profitable for the member firm to work with, not against, the choreographer. As we've seen, the choreographer provides great value to member firms in acquiring customers, retaining customers, structuring relationships, keeping employees, helping to identify the product solution, and so forth. The greater the value the choreographer provides to member firms, the less likely they will want to do business in other communities that seek to satisfy similar needs.

Circles has a particularly interesting information challenge. Although it has a direct relationship with the consumer and knows how to satisfy the consumer's personal needs, the member firms in many cases have greater physical contact with the consumer. They actually touch the consumer. In some instances, they are in the consumer's home. Thus, there is much the member firms know or could know about the consumer that doesn't necessarily make it into Circles' databases. Over time, the company will likely develop processes and protocols that allow it to collect such information and aggregate it with the rest of the data, interpret it, and give it (sell it) back to their member firms to help them run their businesses more profitably. At the moment, it is a lost data and revenue opportunity.

Of course, even when Circles has multiple millions of members, the value of the information and the partnership it offers to its member firms will be different for each. In general, the value will depend on how closely related the member firm's business is to the satisfaction of the defining set of needs and wants. The more closely related, the higher the value. Accordingly, Circles has different types of relationships with different firms. Its 75 "partners" have much different relationships with the company than do the remainder of the 30,000 service providers. Some will likely soon be using technology to make their relationship more seamless so that when the consumer makes a request, it is actually handled start to finish by the partner. Most likely, that partner will be invisible to the consumer unless its identity adds credibility to Circles. For the partner, this direct transfer of a customer makes its customer acquisition cost only the commission it pays to Circles, which is typically an amount lower than the acquisition cost would have been through other channels. For Circles, that type of a "warm transfer" leverages the partner's expertise *and* people, which is Circles' cost of goods sold. Janet talks about the opportunity she sees:

> Rather than outsourcing, it's networking. All of our flower business will be a direct, warm transfer to the flower folks; all of our ticket business will go direct to our ticket folks; and so to the extent that there still needs to be humans, let it be [our partners'] humans because they *have* humans. Also, because there will always be humans in spite of the Web, we will connect the network and leverage their expertise. They'll be an invisible part of Circles except in cases where their brand will help our brand.

If our partner pays for the lead *and* carries the cost of fulfilling the order, we not only get rid of a huge chunk of cost; where our partner previously had a customer acquisition cost of $100, it is now $5.

Thus, because the choreographer builds the Collaborative Community by bringing together specialists (member firms with core skills), in many instances those member firms assume responsibility for the costs of the competencies they bring to the community. For example, because Circles assumes the cost of acquiring corporate customers and brings consumers to the service providers, it therefore lowers the service providers' customer acquisition costs. In other instances where a member firm that has expertise in filling an order such as theater tickets assumes that cost, Circles' cost of order fulfillment is thereby lowered. Consequently, because member firms (including the choreographer) are able to shift to other member firms costs that they would normally incur if operating on their own, each member firm is able to reduce its total costs and therefore operate more profitably than otherwise possible.

In addition, the choreographer has to identify its own revenue streams and profit formula. And the reality of the revenue streams is that, ideally, the choreographer should derive revenue from everyone in the community. That's right. The choreographer wants to derive revenue from every consumer and from every member firm. Deriving revenue from the member firms is a question of identifying the value proposition that the choreographer brings

> The choreographer wants to derive revenue from every consumer and from every member firm.

to any given member. If the choreographer can go to a member firm that handles the shipping and say, "I will give you information that will allow you to better manage your purchasing and inventory costs; and in return for receiving that information, you will pay me an agreed upon amount and have the opportunity to profitably participate in the community," the shipper will opt in as long as the revenues from the opportunity outweigh the fees. So it's important for the choreographer to understand how best to use its access to information to help determine the proper ratio between the fee and the revenue opportunity, always remembering that member firms must make a profit or they will opt out of the community, thus weakening the entire community.

For member firms, choreographers offer many advantages, particularly in terms of the sharing of the cost of operations that touch the customer, as we've seen with acquisition, fulfillment, and service. This can take the form of offering publicity and advertising services; database analysis; software; professional or technical services, such as assistance in process design and development; or even obtaining basic connectivity. As the community grows, the choreographer's value proposition to member firms grows in that through its increased knowledge and experience, it can better communicate the needs and wants of the consumer and the timing of those needs and wants. In that way, member firms can more easily determine their business model, infrastructure, and resource needs, and the goal of the community—satisfying consumers' changing personal needs and wants profitably—can be achieved.

Circles is in the process of developing the capability to mine its databases in order to generate additional revenue streams and better personalize its services. In the future, it intends to perform customer trend analyses, develop promotions and ad campaigns specifically for member firms, and develop specialty research.

While each member firm's financial relationship with the choreographer should be worked out on a member-firm-by-member-firm basis, the general financial arrangement should anticipate the likelihood that the specifics will have to be modified as business models are iterated. Some examples of the various types of financial terms include transaction fees, revenue sharing or commissions, royalties, fee for service, and channel access fees. However, regardless of the specifics, in order for the community to function effectively, it is incumbent on the choreographer to make sure that every member firm has access to the information it needs.

As we've seen, Circles currently generates revenue from throughout its community. Let's take a closer look at its revenue model:

Corporate Customers

1. An annual access fee per eligible user to provide access to the Circles' e-services portal
2. Personal assistant (PA) access fees based on usage or utilization of PAs
3. Premium fees for use of local errand-running network

Consumer Members

1. Annual subscription for PA access such as a cell phone contract
2. A la carte access fees such as a prepaid phone card
3. A copayment for errand running and specialized services such as wedding planning (Currently, most corporate customers fully or highly subsidize Circles' services, so members are asked to pay only the copayment).

Service Provider Partners

1. A commission on each transaction completed (The company is considering channel access fees in order to join the Circles' roster of preferred providers and a referral fee program for smaller vendors.)

While the specific flow of money, information, and products between and among constituents needs to be determined on a community-by-community basis and may change as the core processes are iterated, we can nevertheless gain insight into the general nature of these relationships by looking at the relationships Circles has with its community, as depicted in Figure 10.2. (The information flows are represented as dotted arrows in the diagram.)

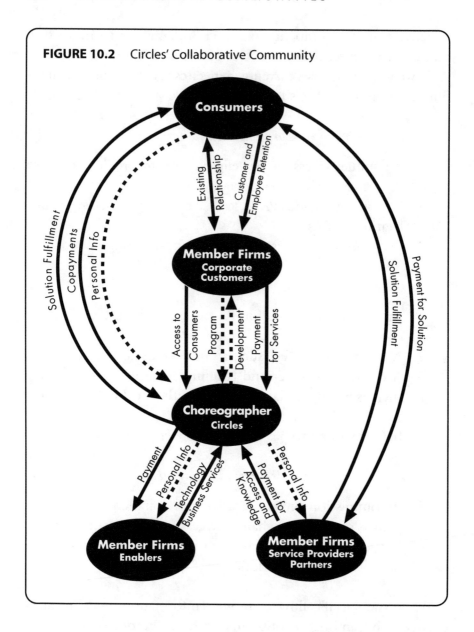

FIGURE 10.2   Circles' Collaborative Community

Of course, financial relationships again bring up the issue of trust. Operating within a Collaborative Community requires member firms to share much more information, including financial information, than they are most likely accustomed to. Consequently, the information infrastructure the choreographer puts in place *must* provide the level of security that member firms will insist on as a condition for their participation.

In addition, the choreographer has to work with each firm to help the firm assess the overall profit potential in relation to the scale of the opportunity. The choreographer, working with the member firms, has to evaluate whether the satisfaction of consumers, at whatever level of need, affords a significant enough scale of business to attract member firms. In other words, a company won't be interested in being a member firm, even if it can do so profitably, if the overall magnitude of the opportunity is not consistent with its own growth objectives. The opportunity may be too small to attract the member firms needed by the community to function effectively. In that case, the choreographer will need to return to the needs and wants continuum and reassess the level of specificity of the needs and wants it intends to satisfy. As we said, it's an iterative process that works toward the right level of balance.

Facilities: Identify the choreographer's facility requirements. As part of structuring the business and financial relationships with the member firms brought into the community, the choreographer needs to identify and secure its own facility requirements as well. Mindful of the criteria of iterability and cost, the choreographer should make an effort to limit any commitments that may constrain its ability to iterate as and when needed. As with many of the other decisions the choreographer makes in putting the community together, it is important, especially during the initial customer interaction cycles, that fixed-cost obligations are limited because of their inherent inflexibility.

Just as a side note—the very, very first business plan Janet Kraus wrote was for a dog walking service. In homage to that, the lease for their current facilities permits four dogs in the premises. We know that took some negotiating skill.

Business systems and operating processes: Identify and develop these systems and processes. In addition to the three core business processes talked about in Chapter 9, the choreographer has to also identify, develop, and put in place the business systems and operating processes that will facilitate the effective and efficient functioning of its own business and the community as a whole. Included within these systems and processes are recruiting and training the team, financial systems, order processing, inventory management system, and so on. It is also important that these systems and processes be designed in such a way that when the core business processes are iterated, these support systems and processes can grow and change as necessary.

Here is Janet's description of how Circles' order-processing system currently handles a request for opera tickets:

> It depends on whether the request comes in over the Web or over the phone. If something comes in over the Web, it gets assigned to a PA, who then has basically logged into a requests screen. And then he or she goes to the resources that are ticket resources for the opera. First of all, the PA would find out if the tickets are available or if the opera is sold out. And if it is sold out, then the PA would go into our ticket resources for sold-out tickets and place either an e-mail or phone request to find out who's got what the PA needs, and then that information would come back in, would get put into the request screen, which then gets sent out to the customer, who then responds whether they want the tickets, and the order gets processed if they want the tickets.

What is critical is that the operating processes not be constrained or fixed by the design of the software that automates the processes. Technology should enable, not restrict, a company or a community.

INFORMATION INFRASTRUCTURE

Good decisions are made on the strength of brains, information, and intuition. Getting the right information in the right format to the right people at the right time and allowing them to act on it in an appropriate manner has never been easy. However, one of the defining realities of business today is that companies need to make decisions faster, and those decisions have greater impact than ever before. Unfortunately, the overwhelming majority of information systems in use today are designed for a different era, a slower era—the companycentric era.

The diagram below identifies the two major components of the information infrastructure that we will explore:

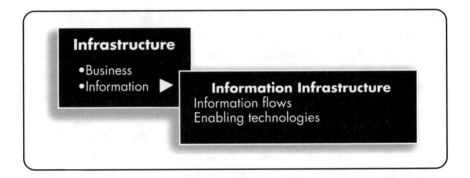

Infrastructure
•Business
•Information ▶

Information Infrastructure
Information flows
Enabling technologies

At its very essence, the information infrastructure of the Collaborative Community has one responsibility—to get the right information to the right person at the right time. Fortunately, one of the distinct advantages of the Collaborative Community is the richness of information the choreographer can provide because of its relationship with, and understanding of, the consumer. Equally

> The information infrastructure of the Collaborative Community has one responsibility—to get the right information to the right person at the right time.

important is its relationship with, and understanding of, the member firms. By facilitating the bidirectional flow of information, the choreographer assumes the role of the "central nervous system" of the community. The choreographer isn't so much a repository for information as it is a distributor of information. As a result, all members of the Collaborative Community can make better decisions and make them faster. Through the real-time flow of information in the Collaborative Community, customers, employees, and member firms have access to exactly the information they need when they need it.

Information flows: Identify the required flow of information to operate the community. The Internet is the connection that dynamically links *all* member firms in the community, allowing information to flow to everyone in that community. In essence, the Collaborative Community affords each member firm and each consumer transparent access to information, all the way from product design to product delivery. This results in a more holistic and synchronized flow of goods, services, and information, which helps to validate assumptions more quickly. Consequently, consumers receive better service, higher-quality products, and faster delivery; and the business members of the community are able to lower their operating costs.

As we have said, for every combination of a set of consumer needs and wants and core business processes, there is a unique information infrastructure. However, all information infrastructures must have certain general characteristics to support the goals of their community. These nine general characteristics that an information infrastructure must have are described below:

1. In the networked economy, the information infrastructure of all companies (the choreographer and member firms) must facilitate collaboration with all members in the community. Customers and member firms require transparent access into the ordering, product development, and fulfillment processes. Customer service must be personal and enable access to the choreographer's complete understanding of the customer. Member firms need to have knowledge of consumers' buying patterns to better manage their own resources.

2. It must be customercentric and provide the metrics that encourage and enable iteration of both the core processes and the business and information infrastructure. The information infrastructure needs to support rapid and informed decision making from the customer's point of view and also needs to support the iterative and intuitive process.

3. It must have the capability to communicate wirelessly so that it can deliver the real-time predictive metrics needed to feel the rhythm of the business and allow all of the businesspeople in the community to develop their sense of timing. Of critical importance is the ability to understand the flow of your business on a real-time basis so that you can react to it and make the necessary changes also on a real-time basis as well. The critical metrics data must also be available in real time and accessible from anywhere.

4. The infrastructure must present a personal view of the community to each member—whether a business or consumer—as everyone in the community has certain relevant information required to carry out his or her role within the community. The information infrastructure of the Collaborative Community must therefore provide each person with that precise information exactly when they need it. Within each member firm's business, team members should have the predictive metrics most critical to their job continuously streamed to them—to whatever information device they choose. (Remember the story of the beeping cell phone.)

5. It must automate all business processes and establish task accountability. A company's information infrastructure must not only gather information, it must aid in the use of that information by driving the business processes it affects across the organization and across the community. In order for information to have value, it must be put into action so that understanding can result.

6. The knowledge of consumers and member firms must be shared. Although not all employees will have access to all

the data and information, everyone must have access to what he or she needs. Just as the business infrastructure opens itself to consumers and business partners, so too must the information infrastructure. It shouldn't matter where within the community information resides. Any member that needs it should be able to access it.

7. The information infrastructure must facilitate the community's strict adherence to established privacy policies and provide for the level of information security *all* community members require. In addition, community members must have the ability to review their personal information to ensure that it is accurate and must be able to change it as necessary.

8. The information infrastructure must be operational without intense and timely up-front definition. The information infrastructure needs to be defined by the needs of the business, not the preset parameters of an application designed without knowledge of the business. And because the business model will change as customers and their needs and wants change, the information infrastructure needs to be quick to implement, quick to learn, and easy to iterate.

9. The information infrastructure must assist with the recognition of the patterns in the information, and this brings us back to intuition. How many data points do you need to see before you see the pattern? With better intuition you need fewer. If your intuition isn't as developed, you need more data. The information infrastructure of the Collaborative Community needs the capability to present the important patterns. However, how completely they need to be drawn before they are recognized will forever be a human limitation.

The backbone of Circles' information infrastructure will be its knowledge management system that is being architected to manage several different, but interrelated, types of knowledge:

- Resources/Providers/Partners
- Customers
- Transactions
- Specialty information

These knowledge bases will track and store information in a consistent manner about service providers and customers and their transactions. Some of the benefits Circles hopes to realize from this system include:

- Efficient management of PA shifts and expertise
- Efficient management of partner relationships and identification of needs for new partnerships
- Tracking commission revenue
- Better understanding of resource and partner usage
- Allowing members to search for resources without PA assistance

Circles' plans to devote a significant investment to provide a robust and effective information infrastructure for its developing Collaborative Community.

KEY BUSINESS METRICS

Beyond the broad objectives of the information infrastructure are the specific metrics that must be captured, calculated, and distributed. If you think about it, information technology is becoming more about communication than it is about making computations. We take the computational ability for granted today. And while each unique combination of customer needs, core processes, infrastructure, and resources will have unique metrics, it is useful to look at general categories of metrics based on the three core processes. Regardless of the specific metrics, the metrics need to measure and monitor the activities that lead to profitably satisfying customers. Here are a few examples of the core business process metrics you may want to track in Step 3 (interaction) to be evaluated in Step 4 (analysis and refinement) of each cycle:

1. **Customer Acquisition and Retention Process**
    - Lifetime value of a customer
    - Number of customers from each specific source
    - Frequency with which customers buy
    - Cost to obtain a new customer
    - Share of customer's wallet
    - Length of the sales cycle
    - Average sale
    - Median sale
    - Customer retention rate
    - Cost to retain a customer
2. **Product and Service Innovation Process**
    - Frequency of sales by product
    - Frequency of specifically requested product features
    - Product iterations until customer acceptance
    - Frequency of product updates
    - Product development cycle time
3. **Customer Fulfillment and Service Process**
    - Frequency of customers seeking service
    - Number of inquiries handled electronically versus handled by a person
    - Elapsed time from a customer order to fulfillment
    - Number of customer service inquiries
    - Fulfillment time
    - Return rate
    - Frequency with which product exceeds customer expectations

Enabling technologies: Identify the specific communication and information technologies to operate the community. As we see it, the most important technologies of the first cycle of the networked economy were the Web browser, the search engine, and e-mail, closely followed by wireless communications. Just as advances in technology drove the first cycle of the networked economy, technological innovations will continue to drive business innovation. Fortunately, as we enter the second cycle of the networked economy, we have a better understanding of when, where, and how technology adds value to the customer relationship.

As we move full speed into the age of personalization, the communication and information technologies that are enablers of the Collaborative Community include XML-(extensible markup language) based applications that "describe" the information in such a way that different databases can communicate with each other more easily. XML provides a standard way of describing information similar to the way a bar code describes information about a product and thus enables the sharing of information that is central to the Collaborative Community.

This programming language is empowering a new generation of collaborative commerce software, a description that encompasses everything from virtual workspaces that allow people in different locations to work together and share knowledge to communications and relationship management platforms to the back-end systems that are connecting buyers to sellers and automating the production supply chain. For example, XML-based business applications offer dynamic modeling of continuously evolving business relationships and operationalize a business's best practices for managing those relationships. Some even include predictive, time-based metrics that can be delivered wirelessly as a by-product of the data architecture, thus enabling precise and timely business analysis and decision making. The software can perform management functions and measurements as well as streamline business processes without extensive recoding. Every Collaborative Community needs a similar platform to get the right information to the right person at the right time.

The hard work of connecting buyers and sellers within the production supply chain and connecting the often legacy information systems that companies use to track inventory to a Web site or trading exchange is the work of application integration software, such as that offered by BEA Systems and WebMethods. These companies are helping to facilitate the free flow of information and thus help companies reduce inventory risk, automate administrative information flows, and take advantage of the dynamic pricing models that trading exchanges support.

New voice-based technologies will make gathering, processing, and connecting the patterns in the community's information more accessible to all. Now that power is shifting to the consumer, the interface with business is becoming ever more personal and thus platform independent, as we saw with Circles' plans for developing its services. The technology already exists to send and receive e-mail and visit the Web to check stocks, book airline flights, find directions, and make dinner reservations with any number of portable and wireless devices. Of course, accessing the Web from a mobile device requires manipulating tiny keys, something that is hard to do while driving or walking. The voice piece of the telephone can be used to perform all of these activities, but the Web allows you to mine much greater information. Why not combine the convenience of the telephone with the access to information and ability to conduct transactions the Web permits? AOL allows its members to access their e-mail, restaurant reviews, movie listings, and stock quotes using the telephone. Voice browsers make the Web accessible to anyone who can access a telephone. While this is already possible, it is a technology in its infancy.

What will all this mean for the relationship between businesses in the community and consumers? We believe it means the return of the personal conversation in customer acquisition, the selling process, and customer service and support. Think about it. If customers can access your Web site by speaking to it, they won't be satisfied with information that is delivered to them from a call center menu. Customers will expect their inquiries to be answered precisely and in natural language. Companies already have the ability to offer live chat—a version of instant messaging—on their sites and a number of leading companies provide it. But live chat means a person on the other end is answering a customer's questions, necessitating an investment in personnel that becomes ever more costly. Mindful Technologies, for instance, permits a personal conversation with a virtual assistant that integrates with a company's databases to provide customers with exactly the right information they seek at exactly the time they request it without human intervention. The technology makes the automated delivery of information personal and reduces the cost of providing the service customers want.

Peer-to-peer computing, which is forever changing the way music and movies are distributed, will also enable Collaborative Communities to function effectively. By spreading the repositories of information throughout the community and allowing the computational tasks to be decentralized, peer-to-peer technologies increase the computing power of the entire community, give each member greater access to the knowledge base of the entire community, and provide the community with a greater ability to fulfill the needs and wants of the consumers. The best-known example of peer-to-peer is Napster, the file-sharing program that was the focal point of many copyright infringement lawsuits; but other examples, including Flycode, intend to collect revenues for the owner of the content as files are shared over the network.[1] Peer-to-peer networks thus may one day help member firms access information about a consumer directly from that consumer and permit the choreographer to collect a fee based on the information provided.

Then there are the technologies like :CueCat (see the introduction) that are facilitating the link between the physical and virtual worlds. Digital:Convergence has introduced wireless versions of the :CueCat that will allow you to scan in and store :Cues, retaining them for when they are more convenient to access.

Interestingly enough, when the :CueCat was first distributed to the readers of *Forbes* and *Wired,* it unleashed a torrent of criticism about the collection of online data. Each scan captures the URL contained in the bar code or :Cue, the user's ID, and the scanner's serial number and delivers it back to Digital Convergence. At present, there is no need for the collection of the user ID or device ID, and as we've seen, when asking for more personal information than needed, the consumer's immediate response is to ask why. Michael Garin, chief operating officer at Digital Convergence, maintains that the company is committed to keeping the information private. "There is no personal tracking feature in the device and in our software. And the only information we can track is aggregate data."[2] As we've seen, it all boils down to a matter of trust. We think it is an interesting way to extend the value of the printed page. We hope you agree.

<www.digitalconvergence.com>

The final activity in planning and building a Collaborative Community is to identify and obtain the resources the community requires. We'll now turn our attention to that activity.

To Reiterate . . .

1. The choreographer has to identify the competencies needed to operationalize the business and information infrastructure for its community.

2. While the choreographer is responsible for ensuring that all of these competencies are present within the community, they can be aggregated among member firms and shared with the choreographer.

3. After the choreographer has identified the competencies needed by the community, it must next identify the specific business entities that possess those competencies and recruit them to be a member firm.

4. The message a choreographer brings to a potential member firm is that in return for bringing the firm's skill set into the community, the choreographer will afford the firm access to consumers and share specific information about them and the other member firms, allowing the firm to produce exactly what the consumers need, and the choreographer will help the firm operate profitably.

5. The choreographer has to make sure there is an alignment of interests (i.e., a desire for profit) among all member firms in the community so that they work as a team, a team that's focused on the personal satisfaction of the consumer's needs and wants.

6. Just as in a customer relationship where loyalty is built by relevance and performance, the longer the Collaborative Community operates together profitably, the greater the loyalty among its members.

7. The Collaborative Community gives choreographers the opportunity to bring together a community of specialists, who in many cases can assume part of the cost structure, making the Collaborative Community more profitable for every member.

8. The choreographer wants to derive revenue from every consumer and from every member firm.

9. Although each member firm's financial relationship with the choreographer should be worked out on a member-by-member basis, the general financial arrangement should anticipate the likelihood that the specifics will have to be modified as business models are iterated.

10. Regardless of the specifics, in order for the community to function effectively it is incumbent upon the chore-

ographer to make sure that every member firm has access to the information it needs so that it is able to operate profitably.

11. The choreographer also has to identify, develop, and put in place the business systems and operating processes that will facilitate the effective and efficient functioning of its own business and the community as a whole.

12. The information infrastructure of the Collaborative Community has one responsibility—to get the right information to the right person at the right time.

13. The information infrastructure needs to be quick to implement, quick to learn, and easy to iterate.

ENDNOTES

1. Daniel Frank, "Peer Profiteer," *Business 2.0,* 10 October 2000, 222.
2. Stefanie Olsen, "Privacy Group Slams Web Tracking 'Cat'," CNET News.com, 22 September 2000.

Assembling the Resources

11

We've stressed that achieving success requires the choreographer to iterate its business model (i.e., the three core business processes) again and again as it develops a better and better understanding of how to profitably satisfy customers' needs and wants on a personal basis. And not surprisingly, as the choreographer iterates the business model in each cycle, it has to identify and assemble the resources needed. This task is not easy. Assembling and reassembling resources requires a great deal of time, skill, and money, but it must be done. In fact, bringing together the resources to enable a community to come to life is one of the key responsibilities of the choreographer.

One of the points we've emphasized is that the choreographer, like all entrepreneurs, is trying to get smart quickly for short dollars. As we've seen, the key to realizing that goal is to carry out a series of low-cost, fast-paced customer interaction cycles. And because the focus of each iteration is to validate the critical assumptions on which the core business processes are based, the choreographer is able to limit the overall level of resources required in

> The choreographer is able to limit the overall level of resources required in each iteration.

each iteration. That is, because the choreographer is essentially only expending resources on activities related to validating the assumptions, it is able to use its resources more efficiently and effectively.

Think about it: If the choreographer tries to build the Collaborative Community that it envisions *without* validating critical assumptions, it will waste resources because some of its assumptions are most likely not valid. Sooner or later it will become apparent to the choreographer (and for that matter everyone else) that some assumptions must be changed. However, at that point it becomes questionable whether the choreographer will be able to obtain additional resources to operationalize the revised assumptions and processes. And if that happens, the business will most likely cease to exist.

So how does the choreographer assemble the resources? It needs to identify the resources required for each iteration and then gain access to those resources. Accordingly, we start by identifying the types of resources needed (see Figure 11.1) and then look at how the choreographer determines the requirements for each iteration.

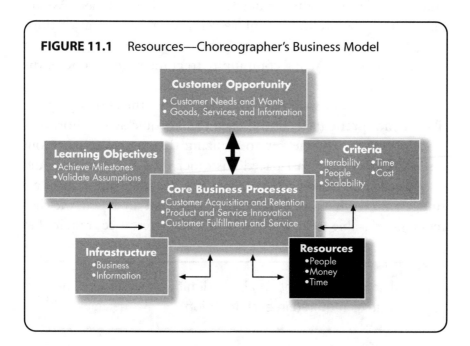

FIGURE 11.1   Resources—Choreographer's Business Model

Customer Opportunity
• Customer Needs and Wants
• Goods, Services, and Information

Learning Objectives
• Achieve Milestones
• Validate Assumptions

Core Business Processes
• Customer Acquisition and Retention
• Product and Service Innovation
• Customer Fulfillment and Service

Criteria
• Iterability   • Time
• People   • Cost
• Scalability

Infrastructure
• Business
• Information

Resources
• People
• Money
• Time

Obviously, the two principal resources are people and money. Without a doubt, if you are going to be a successful choreographer, you *must* have the skill to rally people and money resources around your vision for the community.

However, there's another resource the choreographer has to consider: *time*. In our discussions in both Chapters 1 and 6, we talked about time in relation to developing your sense of timing. In knowing *when* to do something. But now we need to look at time as a nonrenewable resource. Once it's gone you can never get it back. And that's why you must understand how to effectively use time as a resource in building a Collaborative Community. But before we talk about time, we'll first explore the choreographer's efforts to obtain people and money.

IT TAKES A TEAM

One of the points made in the last chapter is that the choreographer has to identify and assemble the core competencies it needs for the Collaborative Community. And just as we saw how companies are better off focusing on their core competencies and aligning with other businesses to satisfy customers, the same is true with regard to how the choreographer puts its team of people together. The choreographer must identify the specific skill sets it needs (the competencies discussed in Chapter 10) and then use that understanding to assemble a top-notch *team*. It's a prerequisite for success in the networked economy. So how does a choreographer build a team to help it realize its vision for the community?

While there are literally dozens of issues to consider in building a team, we think you can boil it down to five key elements:

1. The team must possess "deep domain expertise."
2. The team must be greater than the sum of the employees of any one company.
3. The team must share the choreographer's business-building philosophy.

4. Team members must be able to use their existing networks to expand the team.
5. The internal team must be aligned with the goals of the Collaborative Community.

Let's look at these elements one at a time. First, and in our view most important, your team has to be made up of people who have what is referred to in today's jargon as "deep domain expertise." Essentially, that means it is absolutely necessary that the people you bring onto the team have tremendous depth of knowledge in those areas directly related to what the business is attempting to do. This includes such things as knowing customers and their needs, relevant technologies, and the ability to "wear many hats."

Experience matters. You want people who, in prior work situations, have demonstrated that they possess the capabilities needed to get the job done. Seek people who are skilled in the specific activities critical for your business. For example, if you are building a software solution, bring in someone who has successfully led a software development team. To grow quickly and smartly, add more expertise to your management team with folks who can hit the ground running.

Second, you need to think about your team in a very broad sense. That is, you should view your team as consisting not only of those people who work in the company but also as including the members of your board of directors and your advisors as well as your lawyer, accountant, graphic designer, and so on. Without question, your overall objective is to surround yourself with the most knowledgeable and experienced people you can—and who also share your vision.

By vision, we not only mean where you see the community in five years but also how you are going to get there. In other words, our third point is that it is absolutely essential that the people you add to your team understand and share your business-building philosophy. That is, because you are building the community by using an iterative and intuitive process fueled by collaborating with and learning from paying customers, it is critical that all members of your team believe in and share that philosophy. Anything else will not work.

Fourth, despite the fact that we live in an increasingly interconnected world, most people fail to take into consideration that whom they know is often more important than what they know. Whether you use a handheld Personal Digital Assistant, the most advanced CRM solution, generic contact management software, a Rolodex, or business cards held together with a rubber band, what is important are the people in your network. Business has always been done on the strength of relationships. Here's a great example of keeping track of people you know: According to *Forbes* magazine, in David Rockefeller's 56th floor Rockefeller Center office is "an alcove that encloses a massive Ferris wheel of a Rolodex. This 4-foot-by-5-foot contraption is the fulcrum of Rockefeller's globe-trotting life . . . it has 150,000 names . . . everyone he has met since the 1940s."[1]

The truth of the matter is that businesspeople are often reluctant to admit that their successes are equally, if not more, dependent on whom they know than on what they do. Perhaps they're hesitant to admit that their former boss happened to be the angel investor that provided the seed round of financing because they don't want to detract from their own accomplishments. Or that a college roommate was the purchasing manager at the company that placed the first order with their business. But there's no escaping; more often it is whom you know rather than what you know that opens the door to opportunity. Once you view your people network as part of your team and begin to use it in a systematic way, you will discover that it is more valuable to you than you first thought and will only increase in value when you use it on a regular basis.

Finally, there needs to be an alignment of interest between the internal team and the other members of the Collaborative Community. Other businesses within the community may not come to your weekly team meetings or share in sales goals. However, all of the businesses that are involved in the making and/or delivery of the products and services you sell are part of a dynamic, interconnected Collaborative Community, so it is important that the choreographer view all members of the community as part of the team building the community.

Because building a Collaborative Community is an iterative process, the choreographer's team will change over time. In this sense, building a team requires the skills of a choreographer. You must choreograph your team and the member firms in the dance with consumers.

THE TEAM AT CIRCLES

Let's take a look at how the team at Circles is being built. In the early days Janet and Kathy were the team. And they were creative and resourceful in bringing in competencies as needed. For instance, they arranged for a seven-person team of MBA candidates to perform a marketing study as part of a six-month internship. Their Web site developer, graphic designer, and strategic marketing consultant were also considered part of the team but were not on the payroll per se. They had an advisory board with broad business experience.

It wasn't until the second half of 1998 that they added a third member to the management team. Jennifer Guckel, another classmate from Stanford, joined Janet and Kathy, first as VP of Service Excellence, later as chief operating officer. Janet describes her as being the "third leg of the stool": "Jennifer is at absolutely the far end of the spectrum from me in terms of the way we think, totally! So I'm at the 30-thousand-foot level, and she's at the absolutely micro level."

Jennifer's addition to the team meant Janet could focus on overall strategy, sales, business development, board oversight, and fundraising. Kathy could focus on product development, marketing, account management, human resources, and finance; and Jennifer's responsibilities included service delivery, training, technology, facilities, and service provider management. This division of responsibility is an important step in growing a company.

Although the founders may feel they have to be involved in every decision that is made, the time always comes when they have to let go a little to grow the company.

The composition of Circles' advisory board and board of directors presents an interesting view of the skills the founders considered necessary to have available to the company. In the first iteration of the business—the productcentric business—the advisors were people with broad knowledge of retail, product, brand, and consumer marketing. As they moved to an information and service-based model, they added expertise in Internet commerce and content development. As they entered the corporate market and began selling their services as an employee benefit, they were fortunate to bring to the board of directors (which until then had been just Janet and Kathy) Phyllis Swersky, who was then president of Work/Family Directions, the country's leading work/family benefits company. The members of the advisory board also changed from a focus on marketing to a focus on building a company, understanding the personal services industry, and Internet content delivery.

As the company received additional outside investment, its board of directors grew to include investor representation and a professional director, Hal Shear, who was instrumental in preparing the business plan that helped raise outside funding; and the advisory board added strength in technology development and work/life services. Today the composition of the advisory board has again totally changed to focus on the issues of customer and employee loyalty and the participation of consumers in product design and development. Advisory board members are most often compensated with options to acquire a small amount of stock in the company they are advising, so it is an excellent way to bring expertise to the company as needed, without adding overhead.

But an advisory board is no substitute for the people who get the job done on a daily basis. In the first quarter of 2001, Circles had grown to approximately 240 employees, 175 of whom were personal assistants, a sales force, technical staff, and 11 senior managers with the following titles and responsibilities:

1. Chief Executive Officer (Janet)—strategy, overall vision, and fundraising
2. Chief Growth Officer (Kathy)—e-service development, marketing, sales, and business development
3. Chief Operating Officer (Jennifer)—member and partner operations, human resources, facilities, training, and organizational development
4. Chief Technology Officer—technology-related strategy, planning, and development
5. VP Finance—managing all accounting and finance functions
6. VP Marketing & E-Services Development—product and service definition, partnership development as well as brand, client, and member marketing
7. VP Member Operations—management of Solution Center operations
8. VP Application Development—technology research and development
9. VP Sales & Business Development—sales and business development for both employee benefits and customer loyalty accounts
10. VP Human Resources—operational and strategic direction for recruitment and staffing and employee relations
11. VP Training & Organizational Development—organizational strength and success through the development and implementation of cutting-edge training practices and processes

In a business like Circles, the cost of the people is the cost of goods sold, so the company still has a significant payroll, particularly in its large staff of personal assistants. This cost may be reduced in the future:

The profile of our Operations staff will continue to change as we implement technology and process improvements that increasingly automate each task. Circles possesses an excellent Operations team that can quickly and efficiently find, train, and integrate new staff, while ensuring that the individual with the right skill set is hired at the right wage.

Today, we hire mostly college-educated people who can follow guidelines and are good creative problem solvers. All have solid Internet research skills and excellent communication skills. As we enhance our database and increase the number of partners who work with us to provide products and services, the role of the PA will become more routine and involve less original research. Our PA profile will evolve to require less formal education and less knowledge of the Internet and Web searching. The PA of the future will still need excellent telephone and customer service skills for e-mail correspondence. This new profile will enable us to reduce our average salary and access a new pool of applicants.

The company is also considering allowing PAs to work remotely, perhaps even locating a Solutions Center overseas. After all, as the system is Web based and accessible through a browser, the need for physical proximity is reduced—another example of how technology is enabling business to respond at a reasonable cost to the increased expectations of consumers.

MONEY, MONEY, MONEY

Now that we have discussed the challenges of identifying and gaining access to people resources, it's time to talk about money. In reality, all of the money issues that every entrepreneur has to deal with, whether in an existing business or a start-up, also need to be addressed by a choreographer. So what are those issues?

There are five key money questions the choreographer must answer when in Steps 1 and 2 of *each* iteration cycle:

1. How much money (beyond that generated by operations) is needed to operationalize the core business processes?
2. When is the money needed?

3. Should the money be debt or equity?
4. How much equity is each dollar of investment worth?
5. Where is the money going to come from?

Regardless of the economic climate in which a Collaborative Community is being built, choreographers have to understand that raising money is a *very* time-consuming process. And time is a precious resource, so the choreographer needs to carefully manage the time it spends raising money. That's because, when focused on raising money, the choreographer is not focused on building the community. Consequently, the choreographer has to strike a balance between the money needed to fund any given interaction cycle with the time required to raise additional money for subsequent cycles.

Given that the choreographer is building the Collaborative Community using the iterative process, ideally it should raise only the money needed for the current cycle. However, the realities of the funding process are such that the choreographer must factor into the length of time of the current cycle the anticipated time required to raise money for the next cycle. For example, if the choreographer anticipates that the current cycle will take approximately 6 months to validate assumptions, but it expects that it could take 6 to 9 months to raise money for the next cycle, it has to make sure its current cycle's funding covers the full 15 months.

In reality, the choreographer needn't wait to the end of the validation process before it starts to raise money for the next cycle. Once it's apparent the community will achieve the milestones established for the current cycle, the choreographer should start the funding process for the next cycle. And like all entrepreneurs, the choreographer must make sure that it never runs out of money.

One of the differences about the Collaborative Community, however, is that the choreographer has the potential to leverage the member firms in the community to obtain the capital to build and operate the community. For example, one choreographer we know, who is building a Collaborative Community to address certain needs of beauty salons and day spas as well as the manufacturers and distributors who sell to them, has managed to fund the development of the community with capital provided by the distributors of beauty products. And it might not be just a capital investment that member firms provide. We know of another choreographer who is getting his business off the ground by having member firms pay it for providing them with the technology they need to participate in the community. Another is preselling subscriptions. It makes perfect sense that the member firms in a community provide the funding. After all, they have a vested interest in the success of the community.

While Circles has so far been successful at raising financing from traditional sources (first, family and friends; then professional angel investors; and most recently venture capital firms), it exists today because its first corporate customer was willing to put some money down up front. Janet explains: "We figured if we could get them to pay us $20,000 to do this, we'd be in business for three months. And then if we could get somebody else to pay us, we could be in business for three more months."

We wonder if the fact that their first corporate customer was Janet's former employer had anything to do with that corporation's decision to buy Circles' services. See, whom you know is just as important as what you know.

However, we don't want to leave you with the impression that the choreographer will forever need to raise money. By following the iterative process, the choreographer should achieve profitability and fund the continued growth of the Collaborative Community with the resources its activities generate. Again, Circles expects to be profitable mid-2001.

TIME, THE FINITE RESOURCE

Now it's time to talk about time. The choreographer must effectively use time as a resource in building a Collaborative Community. As we said, one of the challenges facing a choreographer is to "get smart quickly for short dollars." The reason the choreographer needs to do it "quickly" is because the longer it takes, the more it costs and the greater the likelihood that another choreographer will grab its customers. This is not to say that getting there first is the goal. As we discussed in Chapter 3, the so-called first-mover advantage is not always valid; just ask those pioneers. However, we do not mean to imply there are no advantages to getting to the market first. Sure there are. But you need to be the first to get to the market with the product *best* able to satisfy your customers.

The second aspect of time is that it is important to understand that customers' needs and wants change over time. And because they change, what satisfies them today may not satisfy them tomorrow. The business landscape is littered with the carcasses of many once successful companies. Remember, success is never final.

And, while we're on the subject of time, even with all the emphasis placed on the strategic importance of speed, of doing things in "real time," it's not just speed that is important. It's doing things at the right time. Moving fast is vital so that when an opportunity appears we can take advantage of it, but just the raw ability to move quickly is useless unless one has the ability to move when it is the right time to move.

Saving time does not require speed. You save time when you move at the right time. Learning to feel the rhythm of your business helps you know when it's time to act. Like the grocer, don't wait until the end of the day to read the cash register printout. By keeping your finger on the pulse of your business, you have a greater chance of moving at the right time, which will save you a great deal of time and money later. But it means your business requires a great deal of your attention. And if you remember, love and attention are key in learning to feel the rhythm of your business.

The Collaborative Community is an ideal business pattern for saving time as it most often involves the collaboration of preexisting companies and thus does away with the time-consuming strictures of new business and makes use of the expertise already existing in each company that is part of the Collaborative Community.

The Collaborative Community is an ideal business pattern for saving time and money.

As the Collaborative Community views itself from the point of view of the consumer, it saves time in structuring itself to best fulfill the needs and wants of its customers. If you remember, the first iteration of Circles' business was from the point of view of marketing profiles. This led the company to have too narrow a focus and it had to iterate its business again before it found the right customer. If the company had considered itself from the beginning from the point of view of the customer, it might have saved itself one iteration, which can translate into months and hundreds of thousands of dollars.

In addition, when a company looks at itself as a Collaborative Community and considers the customer as part of its community, it can validate its assumptions more quickly because it naturally allows more input from the customer. Talking to customers is not a waste of time, no matter how senior an executive you are. Talking to customers is the best and fastest way to find out how to satisfy your customers' needs and wants and is the only way to be successful in the networked economy.

PUTTING IT ALL TOGETHER

Now that we've discussed how the choreographer identifies and gains access to the resources needed to build its Collaborative Community, it's time to put all of the elements of the choreographer's business model back together, as shown in Figure 11.2. Even though we have discussed the model in a piece-by-piece fashion, the choreographer needs to understand how the individual components of the model are interrelated. As we've seen, the process of building a successful Collaborative Community starts with defining the customer opportunity and then iteratively develop-

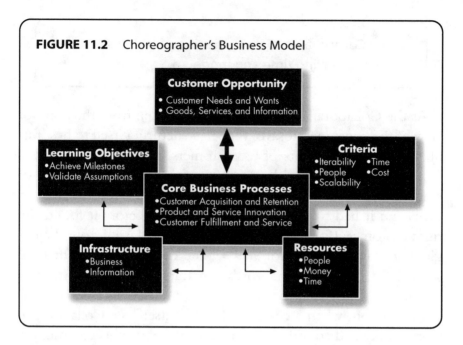

FIGURE 11.2   Choreographer's Business Model

ing the core business processes and underlying infrastructure through which the community intends to profitably satisfy that opportunity.

In this part of the book, we have examined how Janet and her team at Circles have intuitively iterated their business model so that it increasingly resembles that of a Collaborative Community. Because we have told their story in pieces, we thought that the description used in their September 2000 business plan would provide a good overview of the company as a whole:

> Circles is the leading provider of Web-based personal assistance to companies that are seeking to capture and enhance the loyalty of their customers and employees.
>
> Loyalty of both employees and customers is one of the most powerful drivers of business today. The lack of loyalty from these two constituent groups is not only painful, it is expensive. Companies spend billions of dollars every year in an ongoing effort to build loyalty—also known as barriers to exit—with their customers and employees.

Founded in 1997 to help companies in their efforts to enhance their customer and employee loyalty, Circles delivers a unique and valuable solution that addresses the needs of professionals who value their time. Circles' combination of high technology, proprietary knowledge, best-in-class partners, and high-touch personal assistance enables end users to reliably complete simple, complex, and unique tasks—from vacation planning and gift buying to service provider procurement and local errands.

Today Circles' Web-based and (shortly) wireless personal services solution is available to over 1.2 million members in over 60 of the nation's leading companies.

Circles plays at the intersection of three very large and growing powerful industry segments—loyalty and CRM services, human capital management and resource outsourcing, and personal and e-services. The demand for Circles' unique and scalable solution is large and puts the company in a position to transform and dominate the loyalty market.

Over the next 12 months, Circles will continue to scale the business to meet client and member demands. Circles is aggressively rolling out improved technologies that automate more transactions to increase scalability, generate higher gross margin, and reduce costs without compromising our level of exceptional customer service. And every day, as Circles learns more about *both* its brand-name corporate customers and the individual members, the Company is building its own "barriers to exit" with both constituencies—by being able to proactively and appropriately offer the next needed product/service.

That's the approach required for success in the networked economy.

To Reiterate . . .

1. The choreographer must first identify the resources required (people, money, and time) for each iteration and then gain access to those resources.

2. Because the focus of each iteration is to validate the critical assumptions on which the core business processes are based, the choreographer is able to limit the overall level of resources required in each iteration.

3. Because all of the businesses that are involved in the making and/or delivery of the products and services you sell to the consumer are part of a dynamic, interconnected Collaborative Community, it is important that the choreographer view all members of the community as part of the team that is building the community.

4. The choreographer has to strike a balance between the money needed to fund any given interaction cycle with the time required to raise additional money for subsequent cycles.

5. A choreographer has to use all of the skills that any entrepreneur does to gain access to the money needed to build its community. However, what's different about the Collaborative Community is that the choreographer has the potential to leverage the business members in the community to obtain the capital to build and operate the community.

6. Even with all the emphasis placed on the strategic importance of speed, of doing things in "real time," it's not

just speed that is important. It's doing things at the right time.

7. The Collaborative Community is an ideal business pattern for saving time, as it most often involves the collaboration of preexisting companies and thus does away with the time-consuming strictures of new business and makes use of the expertise already existing in each company that is part of the Collaborative Community.

ENDNOTE

1. Robert Lenzner and Ashlea Ebeling, "A Wealth of Names," *Forbes,* 10 January 2000, 70.

Lace Up Your Dancing Shoes

The underlying premise of this book is that at the dawn of the 21st century, business is going through a revolution and companies and industries as we know them are ceasing to exist. Although advances in communication and information technologies are both empowering consumers and enabling companies, they have nevertheless caused a shift in the balance of power between business and consumers that is so significant that *consumers really do have the power* to get exactly what they need and want—where, how, when, and at the price they want to pay. Consequently, to be successful a businessperson must now sit in the customer's chair. And this leads to a very different business pattern than the pattern that results when you sit in the CEO's chair.

So our goal in writing this book is to answer the trillion-dollar question:

> In an era when a powerful consumer is demanding personalized goods and services, what is the business pattern best suited to profitably satisfy that consumer's needs and wants?

We call that business pattern the Collaborative Community, a community where each member benefits by focusing on profitably satisfying the personal needs and wants of a consumer group with shared interests (see Figure 12.1).

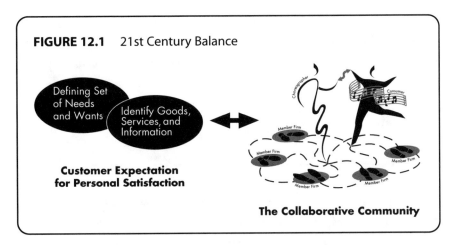

FIGURE 12.1   21st Century Balance

The choreographer is the entrepreneur of the Collaborative Community and builds the community around a mindset that is focused on achieving and maintaining success and rooted in what we call the four building blocks of business—process, customers, information, and timing.

To be successful requires the choreographer to put into place a methodology based on these building blocks. That methodology is *iteration*. It is attempting to satisfy the consumers' needs and wants, testing the business model in the marketplace, learning from the test, and then refining the business model to more accurately fulfill the consumers' needs and wants. It is our belief that knowledge of this iterative and intuitive process through which a stream of innovative business models flows, along with the ability to translate that knowledge into effective collaboration, is the *only sustainable advantage* in this period of profound economic transition.

Indeed, the iterative process of building a business has always been the only sustainable competitive advantage. Monopolies, patents, and other market protections and advantages all eventually end. The slower the introduction of technology, the longer competitive advantages last. But in a time of rapid technological innovation such as our own, it quickly becomes clear that the only truly lasting competitive advantage is the ability to implement the iterative process of building a business.

Fortunately, iteration is a skill that can be learned and improved upon. And that skill must become one of your core competencies if you want to succeed in the networked economy.

> Iteration is a skill that can be learned and improved upon.

As can be seen in Figure 12.2, we have overlaid a representation of the steps of the iterative process (refer to Figure 6.2) on top of the choreographer's business model to emphasize the importance of iterating the business model when and as needed. Combining the choreographer's business model with the iterative

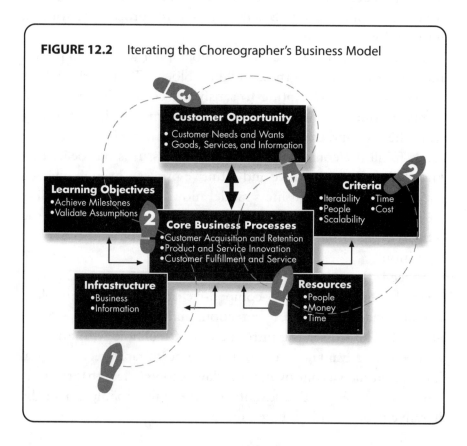

FIGURE 12.2   Iterating the Choreographer's Business Model

process is the only way in which a choreographer can build and maintain a successful Collaborative Community.

Business has always been a paradox. It is about making profits, yet at the same time it is about satisfying customers. On one level, these two goals seem to conflict. Making profits requires tough, cost-effective decisions about time, people, and materials. On the other hand, creating a product that will sell requires meeting and exceeding the expectations of customers. At its essence, to succeed business must try to find the way to balance these two goals. The Industrial Age used the technological tools it had available to

> Combining the choreographer's business model with the iterative process is the only way to build and maintain a successful Collaborative Community.

combine these goals by satisfying customers through mass production. As time advanced, the technical know-how of the age of mass customization dramatically raised the ability of business to increase customer satisfaction. Now, as we enter the age of instantaneous worldwide communication networks, many businesses fear that because of global competition and ever-increasing customer expectations, the business model that will allow them to find the right balance between profits and expectations is simply not there. But that is not the case. Technology always increases customer expectations yet at the same time carries with it the means to satisfy those expectations. Personal computers, the Internet, wireless communications, and untold other technologies now available or just around the corner are allowing companies and customers to instantaneously collaborate. Thus, we are really on the verge of an age of business where profits will be based not so much on the technologies of production as on the technologies of satisfaction.

By starting with a clean sheet of paper and looking at value creation from the point of view of the customer, the Collaborative Community is the business pattern that emerges. It does so because

> We are on the verge of an age of business where profits will be based not on the technologies of production but on the technologies of satisfaction.

this pattern does not just end with a satisfied customer. It begins with a satisfied customer. The entire Collaborative Community starts with the personalized set of needs and wants of the consumer and structures itself from that point to create the goods, services, and information that customers desire. And as we've seen in this book, the Collaborative Community can achieve this goal profitably. The technology in almost every case is here, and if it is not here today, it will be tomorrow.

The Collaborative Community is not our invention. It is our perception. We are not saying that we have created this perfect business pattern. What we are saying is that this business pattern is spontaneously forming around us and we are describing it so that those who are already on the path can follow it better and those who are not quite on the path can find it. And, of course, as we have pointed out, as a result of the iterative process of business, it is a path, a journey, not a destination. Technology always changes. Economic, social, and political environments always change. And due to those changes business iterates. But the Collaborative Community is the business pattern that is best today.

Will it be best tomorrow? Let's be clear, the Collaborative Community as we envision it is probably not the final stopping point. As the choreographer's understanding of how to balance the needs of consumers with the needs of member firms deepens, the structure of the community will iterate. However, as you can see in Figure 12.3, by combining your understanding of the Collaborative Community and the iterative process with technological tools, you can and will achieve success. This means that Janet and Kathy at Circles, like all choreographers, must never stop the process. They can never stop dancing with the customer. And remember, it's a dance in which the customer leads.

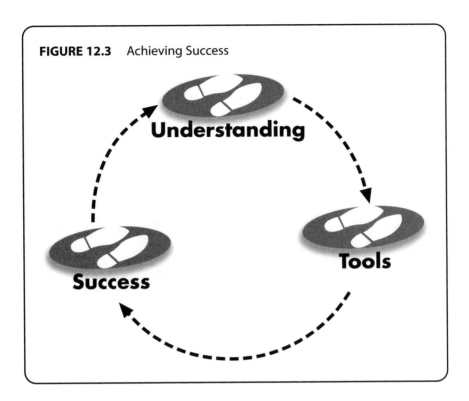

FIGURE 12.3   Achieving Success

As they say in Zimbabwe:

If you can walk
You can dance
If you can talk
You can sing

So the time has come to put down this book, *lace up your dancing shoes,* and . . .

Let the dance begin!

References

Banham, Russ. "Model e." *Executive Edge,* October/November 2000.

Bovet, David, and Joseph Martha. *Value Nets* (New York: Wiley, 2000).

Browning, E.S., and Greg Ip. "Here Are Six Myths That Drove the Boom in Technology Stocks." *Wall Street Journal,* 16 October 2000.

Carr, Nicholas G. "Giant Steps." *The Industry Standard,* 4 September 2000.

Crawford, Krysten A. "Customizing for the Masses." *Forbes,* 16 October 2000.

Crosariol, Beppi. "Netscape IPO Booted-Up Debut of Hot Stock Stuns Wall Street Veterans." *Boston Globe,* 10 August 1995.

Cross, Kim. "Online Customer Acquisition Costs." *Business 2.0,* November 1999.

Crossen, Cynthia, and Deborah Solomon. "Once a Corporate Icon, AT&T Finally Yields to a Humbler Role." *Wall Street Journal,* 26 October 2000, A1.

Daly, James. "Sage Advice: An Exclusive Interview with Peter Drucker." *Business 2.0,* 22 August 2000.

de Geus, Arie. *The Living Company* (Boston: Harvard Business School Press, 1997).

Ellis, John. "Digital Matters." *Fast Company,* August 2000.

———. "The Future of the Auto Industry Is Building Your Own Car Over the Net." *Fast Company,* December 2000.

Enos, Lori. "Consumer Watchdog Unveils Net Conduct Code," 25 October 2000; <www.ecommercetimes.com/news/articles2000/001025-1.shtml>.

Frank, Daniel. "Peer Profiteer." *Business 2.0,* 10 October 2000.

Gates, Bill. "A Future as Big as Your In-Box." *Business 2.0,* 26 September 2000.

Glasser, Jeff. "Investors Eager to Cash In on Internet Companies." *Boston Globe,* 21 August 1995.

Guglielmo, Connie. "Can Webvan Deliver the Goods?" *ZDNet,* 3 February 2000; <dailynews.yahoo.com/h/zd/20000203/tc/20000204109.html>.

Hamel, Gary. *Leading the Revolution.* (Boston: Harvard Business School Press, 2000).

Ip, Greg et al. "The Internet Bubble Broke Records, Rules, and Bank Accounts." *Wall Street Journal,* 14 July 2000.

Johannes, Laura. "Avax to Sell Personalized Skin-Cancer Vaccine." *Wall Street Journal,* 18 July 2000.

Kador, John. "Delivering Long-Term Value." *1 to 1 Personalization,* October/November 2000.

Kuhn, Thomas S. *The Structure of Scientific Revolutions,* 2d ed., enlarged. (New York: New American Library, 1986).

Kramich, Bob, of NECX.com, quoted by Bernie Libster. "Can B2B Marketers Personalize?" *1 to 1 Personalization,* October/November 2000.

Lardner, James, and Paul Sloan. "The Anatomy of Sickly IPOs." *U.S. News & World Report,* 29 May 2000.

Lenzner, Robert, and Ashlea Ebeling. "A Wealth of Names." *Forbes,* 10 January 2000.

"Michael Dell Says Internet-Driven Growth Puts Technology Industry in Early Days of 'Most Exciting' Period." June 27, 2000; <www.dell.com/us/en/gen/corporate/press/pressoffice_us_2000-06-27-nyc-002>.

Muller, Joann. "A Ford Redesign." *Business Week,* 13 November 2000.

Nasser, Jacques, transcript of speech. "Five Rules of Change for E-Business," September 2000.

Neel, Dan. "Ford CEO Nasser Outlines Five Rules of Change for E-Business." *InfoWorld.com,* 21 September 2000.

Nelson, Scott. "Privacy Storm Clouds Gather." *Executive Edge,* October/November 2000.

Olsen, Stefanie. "Privacy Group Slams Web Tracking 'Cat'." CNET News.com, 22 September 2000.

Orr, Andrea. "One Quarter of Online Purchases Fail." *ZDNet News,* 20 December 1999; <www.zdnet.com/zdnn/stories/news/0,4586,2411982,00.html>.

Peppers, Don, and Martha Rogers. "It's a Matter of Time." *Business 2.0,* 26 September 2000.

Plotkin, Hal. "Priceline Business Model Seen Flawed." cnbc.com, 3 October 2000; <www.cnbc.com/commentary/commentary_full_story_stocks.asp?StoryID=24016>.

Prahalad, C.K., Venkatram Ramaswamy, and M. S. Krishnan. "Consumer Centricity"; *Informationweek Online,* 10 April 2000 <www.informationweek.com/781/prahalad>.

Quick, Rebecca. "Getting the Right Fit—Hips and All." *Wall Street Journal,* 18 October 2000.

Sapsford, Jathon. "Personalized Financial Web Sites Spread, Amid Privacy Concerns." *Wall Street Journal,* 19 July 2000.

Seybold, Patricia B. "Making Changes in Midair." *Business 2.0,* 12 September 2000.

Shop.org/TheBoston Consulting Group. "The State of Online Retailing 3.0." April 2000; <www.shop.org/nr/00/041700.html>.

Shuman, Jeffrey, with David Rottenberg. *The Rhythm of Business: The Key to Building and Running Successful Companies.* (Woburn, MA: Butterworth-Heinemann, 1998).

Slywotzky, Adrian, and David Morrison. "Off the Grid." *The Industry Standard,* 23 October 2000.

Tapscott, Don, David Ticoll, and Alex Lowy. *Digital Capital.* (Boston: Harvard Business School Press, 2000).

Taylor, Frederick Winslow. *The Principles of Scientific Management.* (New York: W.W. Norton, 1967; originally published in 1911).

Vogelstein, Fred, and Janet Rae-Dupree. "Easy Dot Com, Easy Dot Go." *U.S. News Online,* 1 May 2000; <www.usnews.com/usnews/issue/000501/tech.html>.

Whitman, Meg. "Leaders.com." *Fast Company,* June 1999. Reprinted from the June 1999 issue of *Fast Company* magazine. All rights reserved. For more information, visit <www.fastcompany.com>.

<www.britannica.com/bcom/eb/article/0/0,5716,109540+10+106451,00.html>

<www.britannica.com/bcom/eb/article/0/0,5716,118760+8+110116,00>

<www.digitalconvergence.com/about/index.html>

<www.iporesources.org/ipolist/ipolist95.html>

<www.landsend.com/spawn.cgi?target=SCANTOUR1000&sid=0972338953559>

<www.sec.gov/Archives/edgar/data/944458/0000891618-96-001834.txt>

<www.thestandard.com/article/display/0,1151,19351,0000.html>

Index

Advertising, 23
Advisors, 190
Amazon.com, 35, 62
Andersen Consulting, 38
Andreessen, Marc, 33
Assumptions, 18–19, 43, 45, 98–99, 103, 187–88, 202
   customer acquisition/retention, 136–37
   grid, 135–36
   validating, 154–56, 157
AT&T Corporation, 4–5, 87
Automobiles, 72
   Ford, 3–4, 20
   Japanese-made, 20
   personalized, 53
Avax Technologies, 25

Bacon, Sir Francis, 47
Barksdale, Jim, 33
Barnes&Noble.com, 54
BBB Code of Online Business Practices, 59–60
BEA Systems, 182
Better Business Bureau's Net Conduct Code, 59–60
Bezos, Jeff, 35
Board of directors, 190
Body Scanning, 55–56
Boston Consulting Group, 42
Building blocks, of business, 40–44, 45, 88–99, 205
   customers, 41–42, 93–95
   information, 42–43, 95–97

process, 40–41, 88–93
timing, 43–44, 97–99
Business. *See also* Business model(s); Business patterns
   building blocks of. *See* Building blocks, of business
   as consumer, 71–72
   -consumer relationship, 42–43, 66
   infrastructure. *See* Business infrastructure
   metrics, key, 179–84
   philosophy, 190–91
   rhythm, 9–12, 13, 89–90, 134
   shift in power away from, 3–4, 12
   success in, 7–9
   structure, from customer point of view, 71, 79
Business-to-business (B2B) relationship, 43
Business infrastructure, 154, 159–74
   business/financial relationships, 165–73
   business systems/operating processes, 173–74
   core competencies, 159–63
   facilities, 173
   member firms, 164–65
Business model(s), 4, 6–7, 15–16, 88, 133–57, 158, 199–201, 206–7
   analysis and refinement of, 91
   assumptions, 43–44
   Circle Company Associates, Inc., 139–49
   concept innovation, 6

About the Authors

Jeffrey Shuman is the founder of the company The Rhythm of Business, Inc., and professor and director of Bentley College's Entrepreneurial Studies Program. A pioneer in the study of entrepreneurship, Jeff has been observing, teaching, writing, and engaging in entrepreneurship for more than 25 years. Jeff has founded or been part of the founding team of four businesses in addition to The Rhythm of Business. He has consulted about the entrepreneurial process both to companies with billions in revenue and to start-ups. Jeff serves on a number of advisory boards. He is the author, with David Rottenberg, of *The Rhythm of Business: The Key to Building and Running Successful Companies* (Butterworth-Heinemann) and coauthor of *Venture Feasibility & Planning Guide,* with Robert Ronstadt (Lord Publishing).

The Entrepreneurial Studies Program at Bentley College is built on The Rhythm of Business methodology. The 2001 *U.S. News & World Report* graduate school rankings recognized the program as one of the top 20 such programs in the country, and the Bentley Center for Entrepreneurship, an incubator for information technology businesses that opened its doors in September 2000, also uses The Rhythm of Business methodology to assist incubating companies.

Jeff is a winner of Ernst & Young's 1999 New England Entrepreneur of the Year Award for his work in support of entrepreneurship and was also a recipient of a 1999 Leavey Award for Excellence in Business Education. The Ewing Marion Kauffman Foundation and The Coleman Foundation have provided financial support for his programs at Bentley.

Janice Twombly cofounded The Rhythm of Business, Inc., along with Jeff. She is a frequent speaker and presenter on the challenges of building profitable businesses in the networked economy. Jan works directly with customers to help them develop business models and processes that embrace collaboration and iterate as customers and technologies change.

Formerly a partner and human resources director with a regional CPA firm, Jan was often a client's first professional accountant. She has worked with more than 100 entrepreneurs in the earliest stages of their business, consulted with established companies, and served as president of a company that produced and marketed educational business conferences.

Jan is a member of the board of directors of Responsible World, Inc., an early stage company that offers software tools and program development support to create corporate citizenship programs. She has also served on the boards of not-for-profit organizations that promote entrepreneurship as a means out of poverty for women and was a delegate to the 1997 Microcredit Summit. In 1998 she was named the Small Business Administration's Accountant Advocate of the Year for New England.

David Rottenberg is the editor for The Rhythm of Business, Inc., and contributor to *The Rhythm of Business: The Key to Building and Running Successful Companies*. He has also worked as a freelance author and has written business profiles for *Boston Magazine* as well as articles for various other major magazines and newspapers.

The Rhythm of Business, Inc., helps entrepreneurs and entrepreneurial companies achieve and maintain success through the development and implementation of collaborative business models and processes that can iterate as customers and technologies change. Through educational and training offerings, consulting, and software products, the company offers the understanding and tools required for success in today's economic environment where advances in communication and information technologies are shifting power to consumers. The Rhythm of Business serves customers from its location in Newton, Massachusetts.